Praise for
Donor Family Matters

"Wendy Kramer's memoir—like Wendy Kramer herself—is invaluable, lucid, engaging, and full of wisdom. This book is a gift."

—Dani Shapiro, donor-conceived offspring
and author of *Inheritance*

"A powerful personal story, clearly written, with relevance to anybody interested in or affected by donor conception, by someone whose work has been absolutely crucial to the ending of anonymity and secrecy and the shame, sorrow, and isolation that goes with them."

—Barry Stevens, donor-conceived offspring
and filmmaker of *Offspring*

"Anyone who has visited the Donor Sibling Registry website knows that Wendy Kramer works tirelessly to give voice to the needs and longings of donor-conceived people and all their families. Kramer's work has taken donor conception out of the dark realm of secrecy and shined a light on the emotional and social costs of anonymity. Countless people worldwide have Wendy Kramer to thank for helping them find their families. Now all have the opportunity to read the backstory of Kramer's mission: her personal journey as the mom of a son through sperm donation. Sometimes with humor, often with poignancy, and frequently in detective mode, Wendy Kramer set forth to help her son Ryan find answers. Along the way, she discovered new questions, new answers, and new possibilities for kinship."

—Ellen S. Glazer, LICSW, co-author of
Having Your Baby Through Egg Donation

"*Donor Family Matters* is much more than a memoir. It's a historical book documenting how one mother created the universe of donor-linked families. Her ingenuity, determination, and love for her child created a tapestry of which I'm grateful to be a thread. Beautifully written!"

—Meredyth Capasso, mother to a donor child
and blogger at donorrelatedfamily.com

"*Donor Family Matters* is a fascinating personal and historical account of the journey of Wendy Kramer and her gifted son Ryan, a single mom and her son who together set out to find his sperm donor, how it resulted in a widely expanded family for Ryan, and how it led to their creation of what is now the world's largest website dedicated specifically to connecting half-siblings and their biological families.

In the 21st century where the ability to have one's DNA analyzed has resulted in unexpected findings for many people about their origin and where anonymous sperm and egg donation are now widely used, this thoughtful, honest, and heartwarming book will be of interest to many people, including those who wonder about the family consequences of this new technology. It will also be of special interest to parents of gifted children who are trying to navigate how to best raise their child."

—Jennifer P. Schneider, M.D., Ph.D.,
grandmother of donor-conceived children

"Behind every cause, there is often an individual with a powerful raw story. Wendy Kramer allows the reader into her personal life of marriage, infertility, divorce, and her quest to be the best single mom to her inquisitive donor-conceived son Ryan. She has provided all of us a chance to re-examine the rights of those searching and longing to know their biological family."

—Jennifer Lahl, founder and president,
The Center for Bioethics and Culture

"*Donor Family Matters* is a vulnerable and authentic traverse through a myriad of challenges and triumphs Wendy and her son Ryan experienced as she cultivated the Donor Sibling Registry. Wendy's initial effort to support Ryan's desire to connect with his genetic roots yielded an unimaginable gift for hundreds of thousands of seekers. As a clinician and a mother of donor-conceived children, I find Wendy's passion and single-minded focus on her child's happiness and the need to honor the rights of all donor-conceived children remarkable and inspiring. *Donor Family Matters* is an incredibly human and vulnerable account of a true pioneer, passionate educator, and incredible mom. Wendy's story offers a glimpse into the battle between sperm bank profits and the ethical dilemmas faced when profit is placed over people. Wendy's desire to foster the "triumph of the truth over shame" is a message and mission that cannot be thwarted, and will ignite the advocate and the empath to fight against fear—allowing space for clarity, freedom, and perhaps love."

—Lauren Wolff, LMFT
and mother to donor-conceived children

"With incredible honesty and vulnerability, Wendy Kramer shares her story and her journey in becoming one of the most passionate and outspoken voices for the donor-conceived. This true account will keep you turning the pages to find out what happens next. A fascinating read for anyone."

—Ellen Trachman, columnist and co-host of the podcast
I Want To Put A Baby In You

"Wendy and Ryan's autobiography seamlessly integrates the uniqueness of their specific story, including the gifts and struggles associated with Ryan's profound intellect as well as his experience in building a relationship with his donor, with themes well-known across donor families, including the secrecy and shame surrounding donor conception, questions about identity, and the complexities of family relationships. Many donor-conceived individuals and their families choose to remain in a comfort zone of anonymity, but Wendy and Ryan broke the mold with their internationally recognized efforts to destigmatize donor conception, to identify the problems within the only medical field that has historically promoted secrecy, to publicly recognize the unrealistic expectations of anonymity in the era of commercial DNA testing, and most importantly, to show the beauty often found within this version of extended family. Wendy and Ryan have spearheaded the movement to reform existing standards for a new generation of donor-conceived families. As most families considering donor conception are unaware of the long-term implications of this decision beyond having the baby, I would recommend Wendy's book as a must-read for anyone in the beginning stages of weighing this option."

—Hilary Bertisch, Ph.D., clinical psychologist,
DSR board member, and donor-conceived adult

"This book isn't just about parenthood or donor sperm. It's really about sensibly navigating any new territory coming from a place of love, not fear. Wendy Kramer's personal and moving story is relevant to everyone in this brave new world of consumer DNA tests and—potentially—the end of genetic family secrets. It grapples with important questions of privacy versus secrecy, as well as what information and loyalty reproductive professionals owe their donors and their patients. Perhaps more importantly, what is owed to the resulting children? And in this era of evolving norms, how do we define family? I highly recommend *Donor Family Matters.*"

—Annette Sheely, M.A.,
consultant and advocate for gifted families

"The Donor Sibling Registry upended the fertility industry in ways that no one could have anticipated. In her new book, Wendy Kramer shares not only the DSR's origin story but also her insights on the real-life impacts of finding family through donor conception."

—Alison Motluk,
publisher of *HeyReprotech*

Donor Family Matters

My Story of Raising a Profoundly Gifted Donor-Conceived Child, Redefining Family, and Building the Donor Sibling Registry

Wendy Kramer

Donor Family Matters
Copyright © 2020 by Wendy Kramer and the Donor Sibling Registry
www.donorsiblingregistry.com

All rights reserved. No portion of this book may be reproduced in any form without permission from the author, except as permitted by U.S. copyright law.
For permissions, contact wendy@donorsiblingregistry.com

Cover by Wendy Kramer
Interior layout by Lavon Peters

ISBN (paperback): 978-0-578-63337-4
ISBN (eBook): 978-0-578-63338-1

Dedicated to Ryan and his two grandmas

Jacki, Ryan, and Fin in 2016

Contents

	Prologue	1
1	*Pick Me*	4
2	*Meeting Ryan*	9
3	*Starting Over*	14
4	*Boy Wonder*	18
5	*Find Me*	27
6	*Oprah Calls*	35
7	*Please Be Kind*	39
8	*Finding Peace by Connecting the Pieces*	46
9	*Expanding Family*	53
10	*Empty Nest and the DSR*	59
11	*The Roaring Twenties*	65
12	*Thanks for the Kid*	71
13	*Portland*	74
14	*Continuing to Redefine Family*	78
	Epilogue	84

Prologue

I arrived to pick up my son from a first-grade birthday party on a crisp, sunny day in the Boulder foothills. It was 1996. Bill Clinton was president, and Dolly the sheep was making headlines as the first mammal ever born from a cloned embryo. But not too many people were familiar with a procedure called donor conception, a way for women to have a baby using donated sperm.

When I walked into the house, several moms I knew as acquaintances stood in a circle, holding glasses of wine. Through the back door, I could see the frenetic play of cake-fueled kids. The women called me over. One said, playfully, "Wendy, your Ryan has been telling tall tales today!"

"Really?" I said. "That doesn't sound like Ryan."

"Well," the mom said, raising her eyebrows at me, "He told everyone that his mom has never met his dad!" The group snickered.

I smiled. "He's right. I never have met his dad." The moms looked at me expectantly. I gave it a beat, rather enjoying the looks of bewilderment. Then I explained donor conception. I'm sure Ryan hadn't said it to shock anyone; he had just assumed everyone would understand. This was our normal.

Before I became a mom on a mission, I was just a single mom of a bright and curious boy conceived with donor sperm. I brought him into the world with a certain set of circumstances, and I felt I owed it to him to help him find answers to his questions. And he had a lot of questions! He wanted to know everything about his biological father. And if he had any half-siblings, he wanted to meet them, too.

On our search to uncover the mystery of Ryan's genetic background, we ended up doing something much bigger: We created the Donor Sibling Registry (DSR), the largest platform for sperm, egg, and embryo donors, donor-conceived children and adults, and their parents (and even grandparents) to connect and share information through mutual-consent contact.

Founded in 2000, the DSR is now at 75,000 members in 105 countries. We match at least 1,000 donor-conceived individuals with their half-siblings and/or their biological parents every year. We've now matched around 20,000 people, and we're the only such platform in the world.

In retrospect, Ryan and I seem like the perfect people to step into this role. Unlike most donor-conceived kids of his era, Ryan had no dad. We didn't have to worry about hurting anyone's feelings by searching for his sperm donor. And unlike most kids in general, Ryan was a prodigy. Being different gave him a powerful drive to find his genetic relatives.

The landscape has changed considerably since Ryan and I began our journey. In the past, infertile couples made up the majority of parents seeking donor conception. Sperm banks, pretty much the only game in town, promised donors their anonymity, and they got it. But that was then.

Now, in 2020, about 50% of sperm donor recipients are single moms, a third are LGBTQ, and fewer than 20% are infertile couples. The DSR continues to connect offspring with their half-siblings, as well as donors with recipients and offspring. And thanks to the popularity of DNA testing companies, donor anonymity or privacy simply doesn't exist anymore.

Despite the ease with which people can now find each other, donor conception remains, at its core, the same. It's about family: people's irrepressible desire to have children, and the children's unstoppable curiosity to know where they came from.

Back in 1989, when my (then) husband and I visited a clinic to pick out my son's biological father from a database, none of the potential repercussions of donor conception occurred to me. Like many other women, my singular focus was getting pregnant. It became just the first of many times I would charge unprepared into the unknown.

As I raised a gifted child on my own and started a website and a non-profit organization, two voices competed for attention in my head. One said, "You can't do this." The other said, "You have to." I always put my faith in that second voice and gave it my best.

I powerfully believe that children deserve the same truth and respect that we as parents expect from them. Kids need both roots and wings; they need strong, secure families who love them enough to let them search for their biological relatives. That philosophy guided me as a parent and serves to fuel the work I do with the DSR.

Until we created the DSR, I was pretty much alone on my quest to connect with Ryan's genetic relatives. I knew almost no one else with a donor-conceived child and had nobody to ask for advice. So today, when I get calls from families overwhelmed by the emotions of navigating the world of donated gametes, I know exactly how they feel. I use my personal story and my experience with the donor community to help others understand this complex process. By the time we hang up, they sound different—lighter, more hopeful, and less alone. It's the best feeling I have all day.

All I wanted was a baby. I never planned or expected to take on this role as a pioneer and advocate for donor families. But after two decades of riding the highs and the lows of donor conception in its many forms, I'm proud to call it my life's work.

1 | *Pick Me*

I never imagined myself with a kid. As a child, and all the way through my twenties, if you put a baby and a puppy in front of me, I'd choose the puppy. I had always been a dog mom, and I loved that, but caring for a little human never spoke to me. Some of my friends adored babies and had known forever that they wanted to have children. Some wanted many kids. I was ambivalent. It wasn't a hard *no*, but more like, *I'm not sure about that.*

Then I turned 29, and something kicked in, hard. The feeling came from my heart and my gut: I wanted a baby. My brain protested. *What am I thinking? Why would I want that?* But any time I saw babies on television or out in the world, the feelings would well up, and I would have to confront the disagreement between my heart and my head.

Eventually, my heart overpowered any argument I came up with, and the idea settled in my mind that I was meant to be a mom. The timing was good. I'd been married for six years to a man whom in this book I call Dan. We had been through the debilitating war with addiction faced by far too many couples, and we had come out the other side, battle scarred but stronger than we'd ever been. Dan had been sober for a little more than a year, and his incredible effort to fight his demons strengthened my confidence in him and in us.

In May of 1989, we took a vacation to Skiathos, an island in Greece. The rolling green hills, white beaches, and translucent turquoise water created a perfect setting in which to dream. We lay side by side on our beach towels and talked about starting our family. We were so excited, so optimistic about the prospect of this new little person and our new identities as Mom and Dad.

I had known for many years that Dan, who was raised on a farm, had been kicked in the groin by a bull as a young teenager. He had always claimed that he was infertile, but he had never been medically tested. I held out hope that we would find a way to make it work.

When we returned home, Dan went to the doctor to have his semen checked. The results showed that he was azoospermatic, which meant his sample contained zero viable sperm. The doctor suggested exploratory surgery to see if some usable sperm could be found above the testicles. If so, we would be able to try in vitro fertilization. After the procedure, Dan lay in the hospital recovery room, slowly waking up from the anesthesia. The white-jacketed doctor and I stood in the hallway. I felt so hopeful that he had good news for us. But after the doctor briefly described the procedure, he said grimly, "You and your husband will never have children together. There's no possibility." I felt like I had been punched in the gut; my knees began to buckle.

We knew this might be the result, but I wasn't ready to hear it. I had an overwhelming desire, a need, to become a mother. Now it wouldn't happen. Numb from sadness, I struggled to put one foot in front of the other as I walked back into Dan's room. An hour later, Dan was awake and ready to go home. We didn't discuss the results, although I knew the doctor had told him. On the car ride home, nausea from the anesthesia rolled over him in waves, and I pulled the car over several times for him to throw up. The sight of my husband suffering from a procedure that had confirmed his inability to have children broke my heart. I felt acutely the misery that Dan must be enduring, both physically and emotionally.

How were we going to become parents? The only way I could live with this devastating news was to develop another plan, fast. A sense of urgency welled up inside me, pulling me out of my own grief. We hadn't been told that *I* couldn't have kids; we had been told that *he* couldn't. The doctor had, in fact, told us we had two options: adoption or donor insemination. Adoption made both of us nervous, not about the child we would get, but about our chances of being approved as parents. We knew that adoption involved thorough background checks. Dan's history of addiction and violence had created a police record that would make any adoption agency think twice. Even though Dan had worked incredibly hard to heal, going through multiple therapies and rehabs, we both feared that an outside examination of the facts would immediately disqualify us.

We were down to one choice, and I didn't fully understand how it worked. Donor insemination? I had heard of it but didn't know of anyone who had ever done it. I quickly learned that using donor sperm would allow me to experience pregnancy and also allow me to deliver and raise a genetically related child. Count me in.

I'm sure Dan was going through more pain than he let on. While he had always assumed that he was infertile, it must have been a blow to hear it confirmed. Dan's nature was to keep his processing and coping private, even from me. Still, he sounded open to the donor insemination idea; we both knew this was the only way we'd become parents.

The panic that began to well up inside me when I thought of not having a baby quashed any doubt I had about this foreign procedure. We went full speed ahead to the insemination clinic.

Conceptions Reproductive Associates in Denver looked like a classic OB/GYN office. The walls were painted in feminine pastels and covered with pictures of chubby babies. Our first appointment involved tests to ensure I didn't have any infertility issues. Then they gave us a printout that I can only describe as a sperm catalog. I brought the papers home and started reading through them. Height, weight, eye color, hair color; entry after entry after entry—it all began to blend together. I tossed the papers aside in frustration. How in the world do you pick the father of your child from a list like that? I never even showed the papers to Dan; it felt too weird.

My tests came back normal, so it was time to choose our donor. Back at Conceptions, Dan and I sat across a desk from a woman at a computer. Because I had failed to select from the papers they gave me, we needed to make the choice now.

"We want to match my husband, obviously," I told her, feeling surreal even talking about this. "He's five-foot-ten, has green eyes, sandy brown hair, and Irish heritage."

The woman clacked at the keyboard and focused on her screen.

"Well, I have the Irish background and the five-ten." She clacked away at the computer again. "But if you want green eyes, we're going to have to go with five-eleven." Several more suggestions followed.

The floor under me shook, and I glanced over at Dan to see his knee bouncing up and down, a nervous habit. I felt his discomfort viscerally in my own body. I had to do something to make this better for him.

Pick Me

"Look," I said to the woman, gesturing with two upturned hands at my husband. "This is what he looks like. You have all the details. Please, just find somebody who matches him closely."

I stood up, as did Dan, and we walked out of the office.

Looking back, it seems ridiculous that I gave so little thought to the selection of half of my child's DNA. We didn't discuss health background, intelligence, or anything of real importance. I was so laser-focused on my goal of having this child that my mindset was, "Just give me the baby, and I'll worry about everything else later." Our ability to conceive seemed so tenuous, so fragile, that I walked toward it with singular focus, not looking left or right. I wanted nothing to get in the way of what I felt so powerfully was my destiny.

We went home with an ovulation kit, and my results came up positive a couple of weeks later, on Labor Day weekend. I called the office, we made the hour drive, and the doctor came in to perform the insemination. In order to improve my chances, they did the procedure two days in a row, on the Sunday and Monday of the holiday weekend.

The insemination itself took only a minute and involved a device that seemed not much different from a turkey baster. I had to spend the next 10 minutes with my legs elevated, staring at a poster of Kevin Costner that the clinic staff had thoughtfully taped to the ceiling. It was *Dances with Wolves* Kevin Costner, so not an unpleasant experience at all.

I spent the next several days waddling around, my legs pressed tightly together, treating myself gingerly and not wanting to disrupt any potential fertilization. I didn't want anything falling out! I could barely contain my excitement at the thought that at any moment, the sperm could be meeting my egg and making a connection.

Pick me, pick me! That was my mantra, as I lay in bed at night, as Dan and I loaded firewood into the house, and as I sat at my desk at work. I could hardly focus on anything else. About 10 days later, I got an answer back from all the thoughts I had been sending down into my womb. I could feel something different. It wasn't anything I could exactly describe; it just felt like something was going on down there.

Of course, no one believed me. It was, I was told, way too early to know. My mom and my friends listened patiently when I told them, but they responded along the lines of, "Oh, isn't that cute. You want to be pregnant so badly, you actually feel that you are!" While they laughed and rolled their eyes, I did an at-home pregnancy test, and it came back positive. But it was earlier than the test was supposed to work, so I held my excitement in check and went to the doctor's office for their more accurate test. In those days, you had to wait a day or two before receiving the results.

The next day, Dan and I went to a car race with some friends. As engines screamed and cars streaked by in a colorful blur, my mind was elsewhere. During a break in the racing, I walked down to the pay phones. I stood in line for the phone, shifting from one foot to the other with anxious energy. When it was my turn, I called my home phone to check my messages. I had just one message on my answering machine:

"Hi Wendy, this is Dr. Gottesfeld. I'm calling to tell you that you are pregnant."

I let out a little scream, hung up the phone, and immediately dialed my mom.

"Mom, remember that home pregnancy test I took?"

"Oh, I know honey...," Mom answered sympathetically, attempting to console me for the news she thought I had called to tell her. "No, no, I really am!" I said, my voice breaking into a sob. "The doctor confirmed it!" Mom cried with me as I stood at the pay phone at the auto speedway, a long line of people waiting for me to hang up.

My mind spun with joy, excitement, and anticipation. I hurried back to our seats to tell Dan and our friends. Dan was thrilled. We hugged, cried, laughed, then cried again. I could barely sit still in my seat for the rest of the races. I felt like the only character in focus in a movie scene; everything else went blurry. It was just me in my own world of being pregnant—blissfully, incredibly pregnant.

Meeting Ryan | 2

Oh my god, I'm pregnant with a stranger's baby. The thought occurred to me not long after receiving my positive results from the doctor. I can honestly say it was my first moment of panic since I felt those twinges of maternal instinct six months earlier. On my mission to get pregnant, I had allowed no space in my mind for negative thinking. One hundred percent sure and ready, I experienced not even a glimmer of hesitation. I think it's why I got pregnant on the first try; my intention was crystal clear. Now that I had achieved this major milestone, I had some time to reflect—nine months, actually. The feeling wasn't negative, just a little odd. I didn't know the father of my baby. At that point I had no idea where Conceptions got their sperm. It could be anybody: the cashier at the grocery store, a neighbor, or someone on the opposite side of the country.

But the more pregnant I became, the less strange it felt. The baby seemed more like mine as it grew in my body. I wanted to acknowledge our shared genetic history. For the first time, family photos of my parents, grandparents, and great-grandparents came out of storage and were displayed on the mantle. In hindsight, I can see the importance I felt of connecting to my side of our ancestral history as I began to realize that my baby's paternal family history would be missing.

I began to ponder more about what makes us who we are, the nature and the nurture. Back then I thought that who we become is probably a little more dependent on nurture: the family that raises us, life events, our community, friends, teachers, and our environment. I gave slightly less credit to the DNA blueprint that we're all born with. My thoughts about that would tip the other way over time.

Donor insemination was virtually unheard of at that time, at least among my friends and family in Colorado. And in the pre-internet era, I couldn't easily research the topic or connect with others like me. In fact, it would be several years until I met another mom who had used donor sperm to conceive.

Despite being new to this, my instinct from the beginning was to be completely open about my pregnancy. Dan agreed. For us, there was no shame attached to it. We told everyone the truth about the donor insemination. Dan's sense of humor was one of his best qualities, and he joked about the donor sperm all the time. We made it seem normal. I found that if I talked about it openly, honestly, and with confidence, I received only positive or curious reactions from people. It was a lesson I would draw upon often in the coming years.

The pregnancy went well, and with support from our family and excitement about our new addition, Dan and I felt really optimistic about our future. My one lingering fear had to do with my own ability as a mom. I hadn't been around babies at all as an adult. I sometimes wondered if all my maternal urges would actually translate into capable mothering when the baby came.

I took maternity swim classes, and one of my friends from the class gave birth a month before my due date. I went over to visit her and her newborn. At one point, she went to the bathroom, leaving me to watch the baby. He was lying on the floor, and I wondered rather frantically what to do with him. Pick him up? Get down on the floor with him? Talk to him? Clueless and panicked, I felt so relieved when my friend returned. Okay, so I didn't have the mom thing going on yet. I hoped that it would magically kick in when my baby arrived.

A month later, on May 22, 1990, after 37 hours of labor, Ryan was born. I think for every woman who gives birth, it's a profound moment. It's the first time that you're meeting your child. For me, the birth felt like an even bigger moment of revelation, because the process wasn't natural or easy ... I had created this baby with someone I didn't know.

I wasn't able to hold Ryan right away, because the hospital had overdosed me on the epidural, and I couldn't lift my arms. Then I had trouble breathing, so the nurses hovered over me for a while. But once I finally held that little bundle in my arms, he was mine. No part of him seemed a stranger to me. He felt completely mine, and I was totally his.

Ryan had dark hair and dark eyes and was 100% healthy. He was perfect. As soon as we were released from the hospital, I went over to visit my father, and I carried Ryan in with me as naturally as if I had been doing it for years. That woman who didn't know what to do with a baby had disappeared, replaced by a mom. It felt wonderful.

Over the next few weeks, Ryan's brown hair fell out and light blond hair came in. Neither Dan nor I were blond. People would ask me, "Where did he get that blond hair?" I would answer, truthfully, "I have no idea!" He gained weight quickly, doubling his size in six weeks. His chubby cheeks pushed his eyes up on his face. One day my mom looked at him quizzically and said, "Are you sure he's not Asian?"

I laughed. "No, I'm not sure. I put in for a Caucasian, but who knows?"

At that point, it made no difference to me. His background was an unknown, so it hardly mattered which unknown it was. He was my baby, period.

As I learned how to be a mom, Ryan and I had our ups and downs, like every new mother and child. Some days could be overwhelming. He cried; I cried. I would look at him and say, helplessly, "I don't know what you need." Most days, just the sight of him made me happy. I never wanted to put him down.

I jumped into parenthood with both feet, but Dan held back. He rarely helped with diapers, feedings, or baths. When I asked him for help, he made excuses. It was just one of a few foreboding signs in the months after Ryan's birth. When my family had come to the hospital to meet Ryan, someone had brought a bottle of champagne. Even in all the excitement of the moment, I remember Dan picking up the bottle. Next, I saw him holding a glass. I had a moment of panic. *No, no, no!* I yelled in my head. Then another voice said, *It's okay. It's your son's birth day, and it's just one glass.* I tormented myself with worry that day. With all of Dan's therapy and rehab, I knew a lot about alcoholism; I felt like an expert at that point. I knew for certain that if you are an alcoholic, you should not have one single drink.

My worry was prescient. Dan fell back into his old habits. Occasional glasses of wine turned into daily tumblers. As he drank more, he became more belligerent. In our backyard he had built a cannon to shoot bowling balls into the foothills. He and his friends would fire off the cannon even while I tried to put Ryan down for a nap. I knew Dan was a good person. He would give anybody the shirt off his back. He had tried so hard to solve his problems. But now I needed more. We now had a family, a shared responsibility, and he was obviously struggling and falling short.

After Ryan's birth, I had almost immediately gone back to work and had hoped for more help with the baby as Dan and I figured out our new routines as parents. We had another conversation about baths and diapers. Again, I asked him to step up.

"I feel like I'm the only parent," I said. "Why don't you give him a bath?"

"Because I don't want to be accused of anything," he replied, deadly serious as he looked me in the eyes.

My body went cold. What the heck did he mean by that? I was afraid to ask. The comment put a fear in me. It made me wonder if Dan totally trusted himself. It was the last time I asked him for help with Ryan. I continued to bathe and change Ryan myself, and I took more caution around Dan in general, as he had been violent with me in the past when drinking. But we hadn't had that kind of trouble for over a year before I got pregnant.

Then, when Ryan was around a year old, Dan and I got into an argument. We weren't screaming and shouting, but Dan's irrational jealousy was unreconcilable. As I held Ryan in my arms, Dan pushed my shoulders with both hands, slamming me into the wall. Pain shot through my back. Everything had been steadily building, and here was the tipping point. Up until that moment, he still could have quit drinking, repaired our relationship, and gone back to where he was the day Ryan was born. Now, that was no longer possible. *It stops here*, I thought, as I held Ryan tightly, waiting for Dan to back away. I was a child abused by my father, now a wife abused by my husband. I understood the cycle of abuse. You become either a victim or an abuser, and you keep passing it along. No way would I subject Ryan to that.

Growing up in an abusive home permanently wounds you. It goes into the core of who you are. My dad was a Jekyll and Hyde. As a little girl, I would watch my dad through the window as he came up the driveway after work. I could tell by the look on his face and the quality of his walk what kind of a night we had in store. A good mood meant I'd run full speed to the kitchen door and he'd scoop me up in his arms. A bad mood meant a waking nightmare for my mother and me.

How can you possibly learn to trust someone when you don't know which version of them is walking through the door?

Dan's spiral back into violence seemed inevitable in some ways, but it still caught me by surprise. As he backed away from us and left the room, panic charged through my body and accelerated my thoughts. What would it mean to end my marriage? To be an only parent? Where would I live? How would I live? What would my life look like? Even though my marriage had problems, it was a known quantity—I knew how it worked.

My love for Ryan gave me the courage to step into that unknown. I didn't want him to grow up in a house with arguing, violence, and substance abuse. Ryan didn't deserve to live through any of that. He should grow up in a happy and healthy household. In that moment, I made my decision to leave, but I had to wait for an opening. In the past, Dan had been violent when I tried to leave. If I made an excuse like needing to shop for groceries, he would see right through it.

A few days later, when Dan was preoccupied in his shop, I saw my chance. I picked up Ryan and ran out the door. With no time to grab the car seat, I jumped into the car, placed Ryan down on the passenger seat, and peeled out of my driveway, my eyes darting back to the front door, expecting to see Dan running out after us, but he didn't appear. I drove to my mom's and told her everything, like I always did. I hadn't left Dan for several years, so she knew this was it.

The next few days were agony. Of course, Dan knew where we were, and I feared he would come for us. We had brought nothing—no clothes, not even a toothbrush. It was as though my life had blown up. I could only wait and hope for the pieces to settle back down to the earth.

3 | *Starting Over*

To the casual observer, I probably looked great. Thanks to the divorce diet, I had shed some extra pounds. But my close friends and family knew better. I wasn't sleeping, and I felt awful. My life was in crisis, and just getting through each day felt like an epic challenge.

The police escorted me back to my house so I could retrieve clothes and belongings for Ryan and me. My mom did everything in her power to make this time more bearable for us. She cooked, babysat Ryan, and wiped away my tears on many occasions. It warmed my heart to see how much she loved her grandchild.

Mom had urged me to leave Dan in the past, but she also had been heartened by his efforts to get better. I'm sure it pained her to see us in this position, and she stayed uncharacteristically quiet about my marriage during our time with her. A lively, strong, and funny woman who had been through her own tough marriage, she was an invaluable ally for me and Ryan. My brother Mitchell also provided amazing support.

Ryan gave me so many bright moments during those dark days. One day I was sitting on a kitchen chair, tears streaming down my face. Ryan waddled over and took his sippy cup with the nipple out of his own mouth and placed it in mine. I knew that even at 15 months, Ryan was acutely aware of my mood and wanted to make me feel better. So I tried very, very hard to keep my emotional turmoil from him.

As we went through the 90-day divorce, Ryan went to visit Dan once or twice a week. I had mixed feelings about it. I knew that Dan would be on his best behavior—he wouldn't want to mess it up. But it still made me uncomfortable, and I worried during every visit. Then something started happening with Ryan. When he came home from Dan's, he completely melted down. The little guy threw himself on the floor, hysterical and inconsolable. He had never done that before; now it happened after every visit with his dad.

It broke my heart. I didn't know if Ryan had picked up the vibe between Dan and me, or if the strain of living in two separate worlds was too much.

The sight of my son in that state distressed me terribly. It made an already miserable time that much worse.

Nothing in my world made sense until I found us a new house. Nestled in Longmont, Colorado, just six blocks from my mom's, it was a classic turn-of-the-century wood home with a charming front porch and shutters. A little yard in back was perfect for our dog, Kazi, my Cockapoo companion of 12 years. When I took Ryan over to see the house, I asked him which room would be his. He ran right into the second bedroom and claimed it, then ran into mommy's new room. He seemed to feel the excitement of this milestone for us.

After my life exploded, this house was the first stable thing to land for Ryan and me. Standing in front of the house, I felt a sense of calm in the middle of the storm. It was a tiny pin hole into a future that looked positive. This home felt so different from our life with Dan in the modern house that we had built in the mountains. Now we'd be in town, in a neighborhood.

We moved in the few pieces of furniture I had taken from our old house and a couple of pictures for the walls. It wasn't much, but it felt very much like home.

Because I gave Dan the house, the divorce went really smoothly. We were done in 90 days. But I still had to cope with the constant stress of Ryan's visits with Dan. While he might be on his best behavior now, it would be almost certain that Ryan would, at some time, bear witness to violence. If not against him, it would be against Dan's next partner, and witnessing that would cause irreparable harm. How could I possibly keep that from happening?

In December, shortly after we finalized the divorce, Dan and I were arguing on the phone. In an impulsive moment, I asked, "What would it take for you to leave us alone?"

After a pause, Dan said, *"How much* are you talking?"

I couldn't believe it. *I can do this with money?* I never imagined it would be so simple. I didn't want to pass up this chance. I blurted out a dollar amount in the multiple thousands and added in a piece of land I had gotten in the divorce agreement. Also, I had filed charges against him after he came to my work and tried to reach through my car window and grab me. I told him that I'd also drop those charges.

"Okay," he said.

Still not quite believing what was happening, I raced home that night, my mind working through all the steps that needed to happen to close this deal. With no lawyers available at that hour, I did my best with the legalese. I typed out a legal document stating that Dan would accept what I'd promised him "in exchange for relinquishing all rights and responsibilities as a parent." Then I called him and told him to meet me at 6:00 the next morning at my office. I wanted to give him no time for second thoughts.

I was up before dawn. I typed up a quitclaim deed for the piece of land and was able to secure the needed cash. As I went to my office to meet Dan, I worried that he would change his mind. My adrenaline raced. *Sign the document; don't get into an argument, just sign*, I pleaded with him in my head.

Dan arrived on time and we walked into my office. I showed him the cash, the deed, and the letter to withdraw the charges against him. He seemed slightly agitated, sighing audibly as he paced back and forth at my desk. I put the document in front of him, handed him the pen, and held my breath. *Sign, sign, sign.* With a quick, anxious flurry of the pen, Dan gave up his rights and responsibilities as a dad, and I had all the paperwork I would need to take to court to make it legal. Both of us dazed, like deer in headlights, we said goodbye.

I stood in my office, limp from the past 12 hours of frenzied work and worry. A huge sense of relief overwhelmed me, and I sat down in my chair, stunned by what we had just done. It wasn't until the next morning that I started crying. And I couldn't stop. I cried every day for the next four months. *Oh my god, what have I done? I've taken away the only father my son may ever have.*

I had faced a terrible choice and made a gut decision. Was no father better than a bad father? It took me four months of wrestling and second-guessing to finally understand that I had done the right thing. In the end, I felt like I had literally purchased Ryan's safety and happiness. He would not grow up with alcohol and violence, and I would be free of it, too. I took back my maiden name and changed the name on Ryan's birth certificate. We would both be Kramers.

When Ryan was 7, he finally asked the question I knew would eventually come: "If Dan could have been my dad, why did we leave him?" Measuring my words carefully, I answered, "Because I wanted to make sure that you were happy and safe." He seemed to understand my use of the word "safe," and we never talked about it again. It was important to me to never speak unkindly about Dan to Ryan, and some things were much better left unsaid.

It would be easy for someone to misconstrue Dan's motives, but I know he loved Ryan. He wasn't a bad person. He had tough things happen to him in life that made his mind work a bit differently. I honestly believe he took my deal in order to protect Ryan. We didn't speak for a year and a half. Then, after a phone call where we both cried and forgave, we started a friendship. I reintroduced Ryan to Dan as a family friend (and my ex-husband), and they forged their own relationship. Dan felt like a brother to me. I cared about him and wanted him to be well. This friendly relationship with Dan lasted through 2015, until he started calling both Ryan and me, obviously inebriated, and belligerent. Sadly, both Ryan and I ended our relationship with Dan at that time.

With perspective, I can see that I married someone just like my dad. Both men were smart, creative, funny, and kind—but with issues. I couldn't fix my dad, so maybe I tried to find a man I could fix. I had more power with Dan than I did with my father, and at times I really thought he'd turned the corner. As a problem-solver, I was always compelled to stay, especially since he tried so hard, through therapies, rehabs, and counseling groups, to free himself of his demons. I had to live with an abusive dad until I was 9 years old. I wanted better for Ryan. I'm grateful Ryan has no memory of that last day with Dan, the anger in his eyes, the impact with the wall, my panic as I fled. I needed to give my son a better life, even if it meant losing his dad.

4 | *Boy Wonder*

After a year and a half in the flatlands, the mountains called to me. We moved to a small mountain town called Nederland. This place, I thought, was perfect for raising a child. Close to Boulder, not too far from my family, wildlife everywhere, not a single traffic light, and with spectacular views of the Indian Peaks mountain range and the Continental Divide.

Ryan, age 2

At age 2, Ryan was a joy. Full of energy and curiosity, he had an active mind and a big vocabulary. He wondered aloud if a witch's brew was soup or stew. He had an imaginary friend named Phil. He was alternately Superman and Clark Kent, complete personas with appropriate outfits, and called me Lewis (not Lois), as we were Lewis and Clark who had also discovered the great Northwest. He had already memorized our phone number, Grandma's phone number, and our address. He used the word "actually" in conversation.

But Ryan's direct question one day stopped me in my tracks. "So, did my dad die, or what?" he asked, his light blond bangs framing his bright, inquisitive brown eyes.

Boy Wonder

I knew we'd talk about it someday, but I didn't think it would be this soon. Ryan didn't remember Dan, so I knew his question referred to our great unknown: his biological father. In a way, I'd looked forward to this moment. It was an opportunity to lay the foundation of understanding his origins. Still, I needed to explain this in a way that wouldn't confuse a 2-year-old.

"Well," I said, organizing my thoughts quickly, "I really wanted to have a baby. And for a baby, you need to have an egg from a mommy and a sperm from a daddy. Since I didn't have a sperm, I went to a really nice doctor who gave me the sperm so that I could have you."

He nodded, then asked a question about choo-choo trains. Phew, that was easy. It took all of 30 seconds, and we'd conquered a major milestone. He now had the first piece of his biological history, a cornerstone conversation that we would build on over the years.

My honesty with Ryan came from my gut feelings about parenthood. I would expect my child to be completely honest with me as he grew up. As a parent, why wouldn't I owe him that same honesty? To me, it was about mutual respect.

Since then, I've learned that many parents hide their children's donor conception. Maybe they see honesty and respect as a one-way street. Maybe they think it's more important to avoid hurt feelings than to tell the truth. Or maybe they're afraid of what others will think. I see it differently. It didn't seem right to expect certain behavior from Ryan that I wouldn't expect of myself.

When Ryan was 3, we went to dinner at the home of a woman I had met through a mutual friend. Our hostess was the mother of an adult son conceived through donor insemination. She was probably one of the first single moms by choice back in the 1970s, and they were the only other donor family I had met up until that time. It was great to talk with a mom who had walked this path before me. She also took an open and honest approach to her child's conception. That evening's conversation confirmed for me that this way of raising Ryan was the healthiest for everyone.

Ryan had taken the news of his sperm donor in stride, as you would expect of a toddler. But as he grew, he sometimes seemed to possess a preternatural grasp of the concept. Once, when he was 3, he told me, "Mommy, you know, I picked you." At 6, he introduced himself to a group of men in my cousin's office by striding across the floor, putting out his hand for a shake, and saying, "Hi, I'm Ryan, and I'm a donor baby." I'll never forget the looks of confusion on those men's faces. The only thing that mattered to me was that my son was confident about his origin story. Ryan has often been asked what it was like to find out that he was donor-conceived, and he has answered by asking, "What was it like when you 'found out' that you had blonde hair?" For him, it's just always been a part of his identity. I worked hard to make sure that he was always proud and confident about every part of himself, including the way he was conceived.

Ryan's intelligence and voracious curiosity struck me as pretty normal at first. As the head designer for Ideal Toy Corp., my dad was a sculptor and a dazzlingly smart toy inventor, having created many dolls and games, including Mouse Trap, Marblehead, Ker Plunk, Toss Across, and Hang On Harvey. My brother, Mitchell, younger than me by seven years, had been a precocious child and became a veterinarian at a young age. Ryan seemed just like my brother, whom I had helped to raise. So, when people commented about Ryan's vocabulary or sophisticated interests, I shrugged it off. This was the type of kid I was used to. Everyone seemed to be using the word "gifted" back then. Gifted-schmifted. I didn't want to be one of those moms who talked about her "gifted" child.

When Ryan started Montessori preschool at age 2, the teachers put him in class with the 4-year-old kids. I figured that made sense, because he was eager to learn, and we had already covered some reading and basic math at home that he picked up quickly. As with my brother, learning to count using money came naturally to Ryan.

In kindergarten at another Montessori school, Ryan's teacher recommended that he be tested for IQ. I thought it was probably a good idea. Having more information would help us make better decisions about his schooling, I hoped. I ended up taking him to the Gifted Development Center in Denver, where a lovely woman named Annette gave him two different IQ tests, the Stanford-Binet and the WISC III. Six years old at the time, Ryan bounded out of the tests saying that it was the most fun he'd had in his life. "Can I do it again tomorrow?"

I laughed. I didn't have to worry that the tests put undue stress on my son. I waited in the office of the founder of the Gifted Center, Dr. Linda

Silverman, to discuss Ryan's results. When she came in, she handed me a box of tissues.

Wait, what? I wasn't ready for whatever she was going to say that required Kleenex.

"Ryan has an IQ of 181," she said, holding my gaze. I knew this sounded high, but I wasn't sure exactly what it meant. I stared back at her, waiting for more.

"It means he's profoundly gifted," Linda said. "He's one in one million."

I blinked and started pulling tissues out of the box. I was just figuring out how to raise a child by myself. I didn't know what to do with this kind of kid. What kind of school did I need? What would I do? I was overwhelmed and terrified.

"Kids like Ryan usually don't find their people until graduate school," she said.

But he's only 6! I pulled out another tissue. How in the world would I meet his needs? We had to be able to find "his people" sooner than grad school, right?

I don't remember much of what Linda said during that meeting. But I did latch on to one life preserver she threw my way: She told me about a school for the gifted that would be ideal for Ryan.

The next week, I dropped Ryan off for a day at the Rocky Mountain School for the Gifted. As I drove away, I let out a huge sigh of relief. *Okay, we got this handled. He's in the right place.* If I could at least have him in a school equipped to handle him, I would have overcome half the battle.

When I picked Ryan up at the end of the day, check in hand and all application forms filled out and ready to go, I asked him how it went. He replied, "This isn't the place for me."

"What do you mean, this isn't the place for you?" I asked, trying to keep the panic out of my voice.

"I just don't think it's a fit," he said, matter-of-factly.

In another moment of gut parenting that would set the tone for our lives together, I said, "Okay, Ryan, we'll find something else."

I wanted us to make this decision together. I respected Ryan's opinion, even at 6 years old. If that was very clearly not the place for him, we would develop a Plan B that worked for both of us. It marked the beginning of an extremely complicated and challenging academic path that continued all the way through graduate school.

After doing my own research, I quickly learned that Ryan existed outside of the box that all schools operated within. He was a special needs child, just a different kind of special needs.

We started out at public school in a combination first/second grade class. I thought the presence of the second graders would put the ceiling a bit higher for Ryan. It didn't work; he lost interest right away. Because Ryan was high energy, boredom spelled disaster. During the class lessons, he'd spin around the room with his arms out, singing opera. He was tested multiple times for ADHD, but the results always came back negative. He just needed to be engaged, learning something, all the time. It was the way his brain was wired.

In a class of 30 kids, the teachers struggled to keep him busy. One teacher commented after seeing Ryan's IQ test scores, "Oh, well, I see he tests well," and dismissed the information, saying, "We feel that *all* children are gifted." Another told me that she would make him the teacher's helper, and he would help the other kids with their work. That wasn't okay with me. My son deserved and needed to be learning, just like everybody else; he wasn't at school to work as a teacher's aide. At home, I constantly tried to come up with projects to keep Ryan's hungry mind satisfied. I also worked full-time and took care of my father, who had a severe case of multiple sclerosis.

I had moved my dad to Colorado about a year into my marriage. As he declined, we transitioned from around-the-clock care in his home to hiring around-the-clock care in a nursing facility. For a man who was a vibrant, successful sculptor and artist, becoming a quadriplegic was unbearable. I watched the illness take his body piece by piece. When I left the nursing home after visiting him, I would literally shake off my stress. I didn't want to bring that home to Ryan. Even so, Ryan spent enough time with my dad to know the difficulty and heartbreak of the situation. When Ryan was 4, he would try to give my dad his range-of-motion exercises. When he was 6, he wrote a desperate classified ad for me to send to the Boulder newspaper for a nurse's aide. And when he was 7, my dad passed away.

Looking back, I wonder how I made it through those days, scrambling to maintain quality care for my dad and regularly facing new challenges and obstacles with Ryan's schooling. All of that was on top of my job, or several jobs, that I depended on to support us.

Ryan and I took on tons of projects at night and on the weekends, to extend his learning. I've always done accounting and am okay with numbers, and I love art and history, but the math and science quickly got beyond me. Ryan had expressed interest in electronics, so one day while he took a bath, I sat and read to him the chapter on electronics from a children's encyclopedia.

"No, no, I know all that stuff already," he said. "I mean really learn electronics, like making circuit boards."

I shut the encyclopedia and hung my head. *What now?* That's when I found Sean, a man with a Ph.D. in physics, to mentor my 6-year-old. They got together once a week and built rockets, learned about genetics, and pursued whatever interested Ryan. But even with the extra-curricular activities, Ryan's schooling continued to be a problem. Eventually, he began skipping grades. It seemed like the only way to keep him academically engaged, focused, and progressing.

I worried about it a lot. But even my most earnest worrying didn't fix Ryan's school woes. We faced such unique decisions, with no road map and no precedents. He should have been in third grade, but we'd skipped him up to sixth, and yet he was ready for eighth grade math. Then he was 10 and in eighth grade, but he also went to 10th grade math classes. Should we just move him up? We did, but not without some hand wringing on my part. I had grown up as a very ordinary person with no talents or gifts to speak of, although I was an extremely hard worker. Figuring out how to raise an extraordinary person took tremendous diligence and did eventually become an acquired talent.

I educated myself with countless parenting books and seminars and became part of the Davidson Institute, an organization that provides free services for profoundly gifted kids. They were instrumental in connecting Ryan with Charbel Farhat, the chairman of the Aerospace Engineering Department at the University of Colorado. Charbel kindly and enthusiastically took on the task of mentoring a 12-year-old Ryan with once-a-week meetings that introduced the basic concepts of aerospace engineering. I also bounced ideas off friends, family, and anyone who I thought might have some insight or valuable input.

Always, my most important conversations took place with Ryan. We made every decision as a team. I recently asked Ryan if he thought we had taken any missteps with his education, as I know it was not easy for him, and he agreed with me that we had made the best decisions we could with the information and choices that we had at the time.

As a different kind of kid, Ryan dealt with bullying in several of the schools he attended. Not only was he the youngest, he was also the smartest, and a really sweet guy. In junior high during his three-month stint in our local public school, he learned to use the back doors to get in and out of classrooms to avoid bullies in the hallways. Despite countless meetings with school officials, we just couldn't fix the problem. I worried about both the short-term and long-term consequences from this type of bullying, so off we went, once again in panic mode, to find another school. Because of the ongoing school situation turmoil, I was very grateful that Ryan always managed to find a couple of close friends either in the neighborhood or at school.

Far younger than any of his classmates, Ryan wasn't particularly interested in joining team sports. But he had athletic ability and boundless energy. He found an outlet in mountain biking and tennis and threw himself wholeheartedly into both pursuits. At one point he asked if he could officially change his name to Ryan Roger Federer Kramer. I told him we'd revisit that question when he turned 18.

We found that most classrooms were geared toward the kids who fit inside the traditional educational box—and Ryan was very much outside of it. After many difficult years at several private schools and the short stint in public school, we finally made the switch to a private school where kids could learn and progress at their own speed. There, Ryan worked one-on-

one with a teacher who was educated as an aerospace engineer. Ryan blasted ahead. Once he was working at his own speed, at age 11, he became a sophomore in high school virtually overnight. He took his first college class, algebra, during that year. I often found myself thinking, *Oh my god, he's doing what, and he's in what grade now?*

It was also around this time that Ryan came home from school one day proclaiming, "I'm pretty sure that I have GAD."

"You have what?" I had to go look it up. Generalized Anxiety Disorder. I got him in to see a therapist immediately, and she confirmed the diagnosis. This anxiety would manifest as OCD throughout his teen years and as an eating disorder in his early 20s that would bring us both to our knees. Eventually, with a lot of hard work, therapy, and medicine, it became something that he would learn how to manage. Back then we had no idea to what extent these issues might be genetically based, not yet knowing about his other donor siblings with similar struggles. It would have helped immensely just to know that he wasn't alone.

Sometimes people misunderstood Ryan's academic progress and assumed I was pushing him. That couldn't have been further from the truth. To me, it felt like he was driving a car, and I was hanging on to the bumper, flapping in the wind, holding on for dear life around every turn. Even though we made decisions together at each fork in the road, I knew that as the only parent, I bore the responsibility. I took every decision extremely seriously, and it terrified me to think I might be making mistakes that would affect his life forever.

As Ryan grew up, and I became less able to help him with his academics at home, I found another way to contribute to his education. When he was 9, we took our first trip to Italy. Every year after that we took a big trip together. Over the years we explored Japan, Thailand, Australia, Turkey, Argentina, and most of the U.K. and Europe. Ryan picked up the languages much faster than I did, but we both loved the learning process of visiting new countries and cultures. It became the down time that we both needed, as well as providing amazing learning opportunities for us both.

Ryan had a great support system with me, my mom, my brother, and our extended family and friends. I have never seen anybody love another person like my mom loves Ryan. Over the years, she took him on many vacations, to space camp, on school trips, and attended every school play, recital, event, and graduation. She cheered him on at all his tennis tournaments and bike races. She gladly escorted him to see the Power Rangers, theme parks, Disney On Ice, and a host of other events that I happily skipped out on.

Despite Ryan's ample network of family and supporters, the curiosity about his biological father that had awakened in him as a 2-year-old persisted. Early on, it became clear that discovering Ryan's genetic roots would be one more project for us to tackle as a team.

Find Me | 5

Ryan's amazing gifts and wild personality made the identity of his biological father, already a mystery, that much more intriguing. We would joke about it sometimes. "Who *is* this guy? I think your donor must have been some kind of alien."

Physically, Ryan and I looked similar. People would always remark how much he resembled me, and I agreed. You can see the similarity in our faces, and we both have skin that tans easily. But he's blond, and I'm brunette; he has light brown eyes, and mine are hazel.

Ryan and I like singing in the car together. We share kindness, compassion, and sensitivity. We love animals and being out in nature. We both love to talk and to learn. We are both highly energetic people. But there is no question that Ryan's brain is very different from mine. On an airplane trip when he was 9 or 10, he memorized pi out to 40 decimals. When he would try to explain jet propulsion theories to me during our commute from Nederland to Boulder, while feigning understanding I'd secretly be deciding what color towels I was going to buy at Bed Bath & Beyond.

A few months after Ryan, at 2 years old, asked about his "dad," I finally called the clinic in Denver and asked the woman who answered the phone if she could tell me anything about our donor.

"Oh, you never received the long form?"

Long form? I had received nothing, short or long.

"You were given Donor 1058 from California Cryobank," she said. "I'll put in a request with them to mail you the long form."

I hung up the phone shocked that such a huge piece of our mystery could be solved with a simple phone call. I had no idea that I had a right to any information about our donor. I waited for the long form with excitement and fear. It was daunting to think that these papers contained information about Ryan's biological father. What would they reveal about Ryan?

When the envelope arrived several days later, I placed it on the kitchen counter. I wasn't ready. Did I want to know? How could I not look? The envelope tortured me, but as long as I didn't open it, I had the upper hand.

That game lasted only a few hours. Then, in a quiet moment after Ryan went to bed, I opened the envelope. I learned that Donor 1058 was born in 1967. He was six feet tall and had light brown hair and brown eyes. His father was an urban planner. His brother had blond hair. His favorite spot to eat was In-N-Out Burger, and he enjoyed poetry. He had earned a master's degree in engineering. He scored high on his SATs. The form included hobbies, interests, talents in school, and physical characteristics. The most striking thing was seeing the donor's handwriting. It made him a person. I could imagine him sitting in a waiting room, clipboard perched on his knees, writing his answers.

He was a barely 20 when he began donating sperm to earn some extra money for college. But his response when asked to leave a message to the donor recipient reflected maturity and a good heart. He wrote:

Educate the child. Raise him or her without biases of any kind. Teach him or her to trust in others but to rely on self. Instill in him or her a sense of humor and the ability to enjoy life.

I took these words to heart. This small statement from a young stranger would be an important influence in how I parented and raised Ryan. I might not be a perfect parent, but I always felt that it was the most important job I'd ever have in life. I wanted to get it right.

I reviewed the information about the donor with Ryan, and we referred back to it over the years. It certainly played a role in Ryan's sense of identity. If he wondered whether his donor ever played a musical instrument or a certain sport, we would go to the drawer and pull out the profile. For a while, having that information helped him feel less frustrated.

Still, it was only paper. Ryan bubbled with curiosity and a desire to meet his donor dad. California Cryobank had a strict policy against connecting donors with recipients. In fact, when our donor signed up, he was given no option except anonymity forever.

We had learned from the form that the donor was from Los Angeles County. One day, I mentioned the form to my friend Tracy who lived in L.A., and we came up with the idea of placing an ad for Donor 1058 in the classified section of the *Los Angeles Times*. The idea was to give him the option, if he wanted, to come forward and meet Ryan. The ad was simple: "Donor 1058, we want to thank you." It included my phone number. We sent it in and waited. A week later, I received a collect phone call from the L.A. County jail. My first thought was the ad. *Oh, dear.* I reminded myself to be open-minded. Ryan's donor is a good person who must have made a mistake.

I accepted the call and began talking with this man. After a minute or so, it became clear it was a wrong number. He was clearly African American. *Okay, he's a black inmate, I can handle that. It's not who I envisioned Ryan's biological father would turn out to be, but ... life throws you curveballs sometimes.* It turned out that the caller was trying to respond to a nearby ad for a Christopher Darden (attorney in the OJ Simpson trial) look-alike pen pal. I breathed a sigh of relief to discover the mix-up. The Darden look-alike was our only response to the ad.

As Ryan grew, so did his interest in meeting his biological father. The long form fell short of providing the information we would need to find him; we also knew he may not want to be found. I explained to Ryan that the donor expected to remain unknown, and Ryan understood that. Yet, year after year every birthday candle on every birthday cake was blown out with Ryan's wish to meet his biological father. (Except for one year when Ryan wished that the Orca from the movie *Free Willy* lived in the reservoir near our home.)

I made sure that Ryan didn't confuse his donor with a dad. He certainly had wishes for both. When he was 6 and using a department store restroom, I coached him from outside the men's room door. When the toilet paper rolled away from him, he yelled out to me, "This is why I need a dad!" Several shoppers nearby chuckled.

This lack was always on my mind, as I knew that I could teach Ryan how to be a good human being, but I just couldn't teach him what it was to be a man. So, I worked hard to bring as many positive male role models as I could into Ryan's life. He had male tutors, mentors, and a perfect Big Brother named Brian, a sweet and playful scientist whom we still keep in touch with.

Ryan and his Big Brother, Brian, in 1997

We still occasionally saw my ex, Dan, for birthdays and dinners. One year, Dan even helped Ryan build a rocket for science fair. In this limited role of family friend, we saw only the best side of him.

Despite all the positive male influence, at age 13 Ryan told me not to worry, that he had learned all he needed to know about being a man from Homer Simpson.

For me, a personal life took a backseat to the demands of single parenting and caring for my dad. Sometimes, I felt utterly overwhelmed by what I already had on my plate. At other times, Ryan chased away potential suitors. Ultimately, my priority was my son. I never struggled with that; I just wanted to get it right.

I called the Cryobank periodically over the years, hoping to learn another little kernel about our donor, or that their policies had changed. The typical line was, "We promised our donors anonymity and our obligation is to maintain that." But I wondered, *What was the obligation to the resulting children?* The kids never signed any agreements.

The Cryobank's policy eventually opened slightly, and they claimed that they would make a reasonable effort to contact the donor with information about their offspring only once the child reached the age of 18. That sounded like a lifetime of waiting to Ryan. When he was 7 and expressing frustration that he couldn't know his donor, I suggested he write the Cryobank a letter. He eagerly drew it up, requesting "infurmachin" like his donor's "phon numder." He stated that he wanted to know his "dad" now, not when he was 18. I never expected a response, and we didn't get one. Fueled by Ryan's disappointment over the unanswered letter, I increased the regularity of my calls to the Cryobank, hoping for any kind of new information. Then, when Ryan was 9, I got lucky: An unusually chatty receptionist let slip that Ryan had three half-siblings, other children born from Donor 1058.

I knew that Ryan would be over-the-moon excited at this news and that he'd want to meet them—immediately. Then we would be back to square one: knowing about a genetic relative's existence but not their identity. I hated to create another frustration for Ryan, to give him another glimpse at something he couldn't really have.

I sat on the information for a few days, knowing I had to share it but wanting to develop a plan first. Then, my mom told him. I was okay with that; it was inevitable. Ryan reacted exactly as I expected: "Who are they? How can I meet them? What if they're like me?" I asked the Cryobank to facilitate a connection, but, of course, we got nowhere. After that, each time I called I got a different number of potential half-siblings. Sometimes I heard three, other times nine. I would later be stunned to learn that they have absolutely no idea how many there really are as no records are kept.

As a 9-year-old now finally in the school for the gifted that he had rejected earlier, Ryan still felt different from his peers. He craved a connection with someone like himself. He hoped that a half-sibling might share his unusual brain. What a thrill it would be to find a like-minded person, coping not only with an unknown donor dad but also an unusual academic path. The Single Mothers by Choice group had been keeping files on some of their members, so we signed up with them just in case Ryan's half-siblings might also do the same. But that went nowhere and also wouldn't have included other types of parents, like straight or LGBT couples.

Ryan and I treated the half-sibling situation like a puzzle to solve. We talked about it sometimes on our daily commute along the curvy, 18-mile canyon road that connects Nederland to Boulder. We drove the road twice a day to and from work and school, for a total of an hour or two each day. Side by side in the front seats, we caught up and shared news, challenges, and triumphs.

When Ryan was 10, we were driving through the canyon on our way home, the creek running beside us, rocky, gray cliffs dotted with dark green pines above us. As we drove into the setting sun, we discussed ways to connect with Ryan's half-siblings. It was 2000, and the internet was still in its infancy. Chat rooms were becoming popular, although I had never tried one. Now people were talking about a new version of a chat room called Yahoo Groups—essentially, they were the beginnings of social media. Ryan thought it might be a good place to look for siblings, a network through which we could have a national reach and instant connections.

As we contemplated the possibility, our car rounded a curve, just before entering Nederland, where the cliffs receded and the huge reservoir came into view. It seemed like a good sign. The world was physically opening up to us; maybe the new Yahoo Group would open up a new world of donor siblings for Ryan. We agreed it was worth a try.

It was easy to set up the group online. On September 3, 2000, I posted my first message:

I am the mother of an awesome 10-year-old donor child. I know that he has at least three donor siblings and would love to contact them. We are looking for Donor #1058 from the California Cryobank. I hope that this board will serve others looking for their children's (or their own) siblings.

At age 10, Ryan had a clear understanding that his donor had signed up for privacy. We also knew our donor's motivation to donate, because it was marked in his handwriting on the long-form donor profile: "for the money." But Ryan still wondered if the donor might now be curious. "What if he wants to know me but has no way to contact me?" he would say. For Ryan it was more about wanting to be known. He wanted the donor to know that he existed and that he was someone to be proud of. With both the donor and the half-siblings, our goal was not so much to seek out others, but to make ourselves findable.

At the time, nothing existed on the internet to connect donors with their offspring or donor siblings with each other. We hoped our Yahoo Group would be a place where such individuals could come and be found.

When I posted my initial message, it felt like throwing a message in a bottle into the ocean, hoping it would reach someone. But it represented a step to further Ryan's dream of connecting with family, and that in itself was worth it. Nothing happened at first. I checked the group once or twice a day and was greeted only by my lonely message. Then, after three long months, another message popped up, also from a mom looking for her son's donor family. Not feeling tremendously hopeful about our endeavor, I replied to the mom, "It may take some time." This mom's donor would, indeed, find the DSR and her son, nine years later!

Finally, we did begin to receive more messages. They came mostly from other moms of donor kids, but also from adult donor-conceived people and even from donors. A message might say, "Hi, I'm the mom of a 15-year-old boy, and we used California Cryobank Donor Number 123." Another might say, "I'm a donor, and I donated in Fairfax, Virginia, and my number is 345." One donor-conceived adult who joined early on was born way back in the 1940s. We began to realize that this practice had been going on for many decades before Ryan's birth and had always been shrouded in secrecy.

It was thrilling to see the postings multiply. And then, finally, people started connecting with their genetic relatives. "Oh my god, I think we used the same donor!" a post from a mom would say. Other times, I would find a match from two postings months apart and email both people. It was a free-for-all kind of format, but it worked to connect dozens of people. We called our group the Donor Sibling Registry.

The feeling of making those matches was pure elation. *We're doing it!* I understood the desire of those donor kids to meet their genetic relatives, and I shared in their excitement and joy. Helping others make that connection was hugely satisfying. I began devoting more and more time each day to administering our group, listening to stories, finding matches, answering questions, and sometimes serving as a go-between.

Donor Family Matters

Even though we weren't finding matches for Ryan, he enjoyed being part of the group. He saw that he wasn't the only curious donor-conceived person out there. He felt honored to be a part of helping them. Every match of a half-sibling or a donor and child fueled our hope that it would someday happen for Ryan, too.

Little did we know how long it would take.

Oprah Calls | 6

By 2002, we knew that our Yahoo platform could work to connect donor families with their biological relatives through mutual consent. But with only 37 members, we wanted to find a way to boost our profile. I sent emails to our three local Denver television stations, and the NBC affiliate decided to run a story. They featured Ryan and his quest to find his biological dad and half-siblings, along with the Donor Sibling Registry.

Two weeks after that story aired, we were flown to New York City to be interviewed by Diane Sawyer on *Good Morning America*. Other television interviews and newspaper articles followed. Each time a new media opportunity came up, we felt so excited, because more people would be able to find their biological families. Of course, we hoped Ryan might be one of them.

The media attention was great for our cause. Before then, virtually no one knew that they had the right to be curious about, search for, and be found by those who were their genetic relatives through donor conception. It was, in fact, a three-way street: Curious donors could now connect with their offspring, curious donor kids and their parents could connect with donors, and half-siblings could connect with each other.

Our media appearances were thrilling but surreal for a single mom and her son in small-town Colorado. I would joke with my family, "Well, Oprah still hasn't called...." Then, one morning, my phone rang, and the caller ID said Harpo Studios. I couldn't believe it. A few weeks later, Ryan and I flew to Chicago for a taping of *The Oprah Winfrey Show*. Oprah was kind and gracious, taking both my hands and greeting me joyfully as "Ryan's mom, Ryan's mom, *Ryan's mom!*"

It felt so affirming to sit across from Oprah and tell our story. She told Ryan, "I believe you will find your biological father." We hoped she was right. We certainly knew we would be reaching a national audience exponentially larger than any we'd reached before.

Ryan, my mom, and I watched our first episode of *Oprah* air on May 22, 2003, Ryan's 13th birthday. We ran between the television and the computer, where we saw loads of people signing on to the DSR. We got around 500 new members that day and more than 100 of them matched with each other. In the midst of the excitement of all those messages pouring in, one immediately caught my eye. The subject was, "Donor 1058?" My heart raced, and I clicked. "Was that your Ryan on *Oprah* today?" Ryan hadn't mentioned his donor number on the *Oprah* show.

"Yes!!" I replied. I waited, poised at the computer, willing my correspondent to respond quickly. I didn't say anything to Ryan yet, but I had hope.

"I guess I knew that when I saw him," the mom wrote. "I gave birth to his two half-sisters. They are 10 and 7. Like him they are brilliant and beautiful."

It happened!!

"Ryan!?" I called, not able to keep the joy out of my voice. He bounded over, knowing right away what I had found. Ryan, my mom, and I cried and hugged and laughed. Finally, it was our turn.

The mom sent photos right away. "They look like me with wigs!" Ryan exclaimed. He wrote back to the mom himself. "I am screaming with joy. We are all screaming with joy. Please write back as soon as is humanly possible."

We danced out to our car to go to Ryan's birthday dinner. It couldn't have been a more jubilant time for us. It made my heart flip to see Ryan's excitement, to watch his dream come true. As we drove to the restaurant, he stuck his head out of the car and shouted, "Woohoo! I have two sisters!"

We reveled in the moment. The *Oprah* show, the massive influx of members to our site, and the topper—a sibling match for Ryan. We discussed flying out to visit them and wondered what they would be like. The next morning, I was up early to see if the mom had responded to our last message. She had. Full of eager anticipation, I read: "We have not told our daughters that they were donor-conceived, and we do not plan to do so." She was obviously conflicted, saying, "My world has turned upside down."

I then had to wake Ryan and give him the news. Not only could he not meet these two new sisters, they would never even know that Ryan existed. His face immediately registered the shock and disappointment we both felt. Without words, I wrapped him in a big hug. How much hurt and frustration was he going to have to take? It shouldn't be this way. It felt like the rug had been pulled out from under us.

The power of my reaction surprised me. I was mad. I couldn't imagine that a parent would do what that mom did. It spoke volumes about the shame and secrecy among donor recipient parents. The shame of infertility was clearly being passed along as the shame of donor conception. How would that mentality affect donor-conceived kids, who now had the opportunity to find each other? This "secret" was simply not the parents' burden to carry.

I have always been a proponent of the truth, no matter how complicated or awkward. Life is complicated; families, especially, have always been complex. Children deserve to know where they came from, and families should be proud of their origins, not ashamed.

The experience with Ryan's failed sibling connection caused a shift in both me and Ryan. We went from a mom and a kid looking for his biological family to advocates in the donor community. It was the beginning of our mission to learn about donor families, what worked for them and what didn't, and move the conversation forward in the spirit of openness.

Thanks to a rerun over the summer, *Oprah* was a gift that continued to give. In August, after the show aired again, the DSR experienced another explosion of visitors. It became virtually impossible for me to keep up with the messages and find connections. Many people found matches, but others were surely missing each other because of the sheer volume of postings. One of the moms in our group created a document with all the members and donor numbers to make matching easier, but it just wasn't enough.

At the time, I worked as an accountant for an advertising agency. A friend at work said he knew a web developer who could create an automated database system for me. Somebody would enter a donor number and a sperm bank, and the website would use a database to automatically connect them to their matches.

Sign me up! I was spending hours of each day manually matching members on my Yahoo Group on top of my full-time job and keeping up with Ryan. The website sounded awesome, both for me and for our members.

I asked two other moms from the DSR to help me migrate all of the information from the Yahoo Group to our new database. We took all the postings and entered them on the new website. The work was taxing, but the only emotion I remember from that time was pure excitement. The Donor Sibling Registry website launched on October 31, 2003. The site looked great, and people matched automatically. It still demanded a lot of my attention, but I no longer carried the responsibility of sorting through messages and manually matching people.

Each new improvement to the DSR gave Ryan and me cause for celebration. It made us better advocates, and we never forgot that the progress was moving us closer to our goal of making a successful match with one of Ryan's half-siblings or his donor. Our experience with his half-sisters had shifted our focus to the larger community of donor-conceived families. But connecting with that donor mom hadn't been a total loss for us personally. It showed Ryan that finding a match was possible. It also gave us a key piece of our own puzzle. Before we lost contact with the mom, she gave us an updated profile of Donor 1058.

The new form provided the donor's exact birth date and place. Eventually, this small piece of information would become invaluable.

Please Be Kind | 7

In 2004, at 13 years old, Ryan graduated third in his class from Ute Creek Secondary Charter Academy (his seventh school since kindergarten) and became an undergraduate student in the University of Colorado's Aerospace Engineering program. This was also the year when commercial DNA testing companies began to market themselves aggressively. One of them, Family Tree DNA, contacted Ryan and asked if he would like to submit DNA. They saw that this new technology might hold promise for donor-conceived people looking to know more about their genetic origins.

Ryan was told the test might identify some elements of his paternal background, like countries of origin. He swabbed his cheek and sent in the sample. The results came back showing mostly English heritage, with some Irish and 4% Icelandic, which he thought was cool. But it didn't help much with our interest in his donor.

Then, nine months later, Ryan received an email from a man named Michael C, who said that the Family Tree DNA website had identified Ryan and another man with the same last name as Michael as his two closest Y-DNA relatives. Michael, who was into genealogy, said that he had figured out the common ancestor of himself, Ryan, and the third man. It was a man in the 1600s with the same last name C. This was a major break. Because Family Tree DNA identified links through the Y chromosome, and names pass from father to son, we could assume that Ryan's donor's last name was also C.

We already had the donor's birth date and place. Now we had his last name. We requested a list from Los Angeles County of all the male births on that day. Out of about 250 names, there was only one match: Lance C.

It felt eerie and impossible and obvious all wrapped into mild panic. I didn't want to jump to conclusions. As an accountant, I'm thorough and I double-check. Despite Ryan's adrenaline-fueled certainty that we had found his donor, I cautioned him to wait.

I taped a big piece of white paper on the wall and drew a line down the middle. One side said, "Donor 1058"; the other side said, "Lance C." We listed everything we knew about both people. The items that matched, we highlighted in yellow. Over the next nine days, the paper became more and more yellow. When we finished, Ryan pointed at the chart with exasperation. "Mom, that's the guy. The whole sheet is yellow!"

"Well, you don't know. You get to my age and you understand sometimes things are not as they appear," I cautioned. Ryan rolled his eyes. He had already done a quick internet search and discovered that Lance lived in San Francisco.

We had waited this long, and I wanted to be absolutely sure. We knew from the updated profile that Donor 1058 had earned his master's degree in engineering, and we could guess the time frame of the degree. Ryan called a couple of schools in California, explained his situation, and asked if a Lance C had earned an engineering degree within a three-year period. He found one. The school said they would email an image of the diploma. When it arrived, I took a deep breath and double-clicked. It was 2005 and a dial-up connection, so the image downloaded very slowly in sections, as if we needed greater suspense!

The first thing that appeared was a date: May 22, 1990. The day Ryan was born. *What's going on?* Then, Lance's name appeared, followed by his degree. It took a moment to soak in. He had earned his engineering degree on Ryan's birth day. As I was giving birth to Ryan, Lance was walking across the stage to collect his diploma.

With this final piece clicked into place, even I couldn't deny that we had found Ryan's donor. Now I went into a full panic. *Oh my god, my child's heart is wide open—this is his dream—what if his donor doesn't want to know him? What if he says, "Thanks but no thanks" or even worse, "Get the hell out of here!"*

All week long, looking at that yellow highlighted list, I had felt this moment coming. I had protected myself with the conviction that we didn't have conclusive proof. Now that firewall had been removed, and the moment felt huge and out of control. When I spoke to Ryan from work, he was ecstatic. But I was sweating. My head pulsed as a million thoughts ran through my mind. Of course I was happy for Ryan, but that joy was quickly snuffed out by the potential consequences.

Ryan was 15 and a sophomore aerospace engineering student. He'd spent the past 13 years thinking about his biological father, wondering what his voice sounded like, what music he listened to, if he had his own kids. I had been managing his expectations all those years, too. Ryan knew, intellectually, that this man may want nothing to do with him. Yes, he was a father [noun] but not a father [verb]. The donor might resent being contacted at all, having donated sperm with the condition of anonymity. He might have a family of his own or not have the emotional bandwidth to connect with this donor child of his.

But there's no way to control someone's hopes. Of course, Ryan wanted a relationship with this person. He hoped that they would be able to meet and get to know each other. He had met so few people in the world "like him." Maybe his biological father would be one of those people.

I didn't regret what we'd uncovered, because it was something that Ryan needed to explore. We had approached it as a team. But I had always known the impact this moment would have on him, and I was reeling.

It was late, and I told Ryan that we needed to sleep on it.

"Let's take a breath and regroup," I said, holding on to his arms. We agreed that we would leave it for tomorrow. I wanted time to think about the best approach. After some tossing and turning, I finally fell asleep, my exhaustion overpowering my busy mind.

I felt Ryan shaking me awake. "Mom, mom!" It was dark when I opened my eyes. The clock said 1:30 A.M.

"Mom, I just sent him an email!"

I should have known. So much for regrouping. So much for collaboration. Even though we had decided to sleep on it, I knew my kid. There would be no containing his excitement; he had just solved the biggest mystery of his life. I wasn't mad, just terrified. I wanted to see the email right away.

It was perfect. I couldn't have written a better letter. He explained who he was, talked about his accomplishments, and laid out his expectations. It said, in part:

Where to begin ... my name is Ryan Kramer. I'm 15 years old, and I live in Nederland, Colorado. I just completed my first year at the University of Colorado, majoring in Aerospace Engineering. Recently, my mother Wendy and I have been doing some research trying to complete my family tree. As you will understand in a moment, I have been missing a large chunk of my ancestry. After much work, DNA tests, and public records searching, I believe that I have finally found the man I am looking for. You may want to sit down for this next part.

After describing Donor 1058, Ryan stated the obvious conclusion: "You and this man, I believe, are one and the same, which, incidentally, makes you my father."

Ryan continued, "I'd like to reassure you of a few things. First of all, I am not contacting you for money, I am not looking for you to put me through college, nor do I seek any other form of financial aid. Secondly, I respect the fact that when you donated as a teenager, you signed up for complete anonymity. Thus, I am not asking for a relationship, nor am I asking you to become a father figure or a part of my life if you are not comfortable with it. While getting to know you would be the best-case scenario for me, the level on which we connect is entirely up to you."

Ryan attached a lengthy feature article written about him in *The Denver Post* that highlighted his academic accomplishments as a 14-year-old college freshman and detailed his life-long search for his donor dad. He'd worked really, really hard, even by age 15, and he wanted his donor to acknowledge him and his successes in life. Also, from my perspective, he was just a really good kid. He was somebody to be very proud of, especially if you were the one who contributed 50% of the genes.

As wonderfully written as it was, that email would have been a lot for anyone to chew: You have a teenage son. He's a genius. He's been looking for you for 13 years. He and his mom are the poster family for connecting sperm donors with their offspring. He's been on *Oprah* talking about you.

I could only imagine what it would feel like to receive a letter like that. Plus, this man was promised anonymity. Ryan's email was not a mutual consent contact, which certainly troubled me. We were Wendy and Ryan from the DSR, a mutual consent website founded on the idea of respecting donors'

Please Be Kind

privacy and promised anonymity. Sending Ryan's donor an email was out of sync with what we had been doing on the DSR.

I reckoned with that by putting on my mom hat. As the founder of the DSR, I advocated for mutual consent contact. As Ryan's mom, I respected his desire to give his donor dad the opportunity to know him. It had been Ryan's dream since he became aware of the nature of his conception. We didn't know if Donor 1058 wanted to be known, because the sperm bank never gave him that option.

I worked hard preparing Ryan for a negative response, and he took the possibility in stride—or at least put on a good face for my benefit.

"Mom, it's okay. Whatever comes back is okay," he said. "If he doesn't want to know me now, I'll jump on a plane when I'm 18 and go shake his hand." At that point, he was comforting me in my fear that this would end badly. Whether or not Ryan truly felt that way, his reassurance kept me sane as we waited for a response from Lance.

I wanted only one thing from Ryan's biological dad: kindness. My mantra during that excruciating wait for a response was, *Please be kind, please be kind, please be kind.* I said it to myself, to the universe, and to Lance over and over in my head.

I thought of all the donors who had registered on the DSR, curious about their offspring and happy to connect with them. Who's to say Ryan's donor wouldn't feel the same way?

Exactly 48 hours after Ryan sent his email, it was deja vu. Ryan shook me awake. "Mom, mom!" This time, his voice carried even more urgency. "He wrote me back!!"

My eyes instantly opened. My adrenaline started to pump, but I felt weak. I got out of bed and went right onto my knees.

"Was he kind?" I asked, looking up at Ryan, my heart in my throat.

Ryan nodded his head up and down, unable to talk, tears streaming down his cheeks. To my dying day, that moment will be etched in my brain. I got to watch my kid's dream come true. How many parents get to say that?

Wiping my own tears, I followed Ryan into his room to read the email. Lance offered some advice, recommended reading *Adaptation to Life*, commented on their physical similarities, noted that he still had all his hair, and offered that he had an above-average IQ, adding, "Smarts are helpful, but methodology and people skills are also vital in life." He sounded nice but cautious, making clear that he did not want any publicity for being a sperm donor.

But this was the line that most caught my eye: "I am thrilled to be your genetic father." In the moment, that was all I needed. A profound relief washed over me. *Thank God.*

At first, a flurry of emails went back and forth. What kind of music do you like? How far did you get in math? What are your favorite movies? Are you married? Do you have kids? Lance sent a couple of photos of himself as a child; the resemblance was stunning.

Once the most pressing questions had been answered, the emails petered off a bit, which seemed natural. Ryan felt completely at peace. He finally knew who his father was, and if he had questions, he could get them answered. Ryan never pushed for a meeting; he wanted to leave that ball in Lance's court.

I relished seeing the process unfold and felt grateful that Lance was a good person who seemed unlikely to break Ryan's heart. But I also had my own agenda for Lance, something I had thought about ever since Tracy and I ran that ad in the *Los Angeles Times*. I wanted to thank him. Without Lance, I wouldn't have Ryan, who means everything to me. How do you say thank you for your child? I didn't quite know, but I wanted to try.

I told Lance what a wonderful person Ryan was and about my journey as a parent. Ryan wasn't just my kid but also a wonderful human being, and Lance should be proud to be an important part of that. If he ever wondered if his sperm donation mattered—it did. I wouldn't have been able to be a mom without his contribution. It affected my life in the most profound way.

It was very emotional writing the email. When I sent it, it felt like 20,000 pounds lifted off my shoulders. That was my one piece of business with Lance; the rest I wanted to be all about Ryan.

A couple of months after Ryan and Lance first communicated, when the emails had slowed, Lance sent an invitation: "Would you like to come to California to meet me and your grandparents?"

Excitement doesn't begin to describe Ryan's response. The happy electricity coming off his body could have powered his trip there. I was so thrilled for him. But there was no way he could go on his own. I didn't really know these people, and Ryan was still only 15.

I knew that Lance was suspicious of me. One of his first emails to Ryan included the question, "What does your mother want from me?" And he had never responded to my thank-you email. So, it was with some awkwardness and trepidation that I informed Lance that I would be coming on this trip, too. Thankfully, it wasn't a deal breaker. With jitters and jumps for joy, we counted the days to meet Ryan's new family.

8 | *Finding Peace by Connecting the Pieces*

When we received instructions from Lance about our visit to California, we wondered if we'd been dropped into the next *Mission Impossible* movie. He told us to fly to a specific airport, rent a car, and check in to a particular hotel. There, we would await further instructions.

Some people are just naturally more cautious or skeptical. Lance certainly fell into that category. The fact that Ryan and I had been interviewed on *Good Morning America* and *Oprah* about his donor dad probably raised that skepticism to borderline paranoia.

In August 2005, Ryan and I boarded a plane to Los Angeles. When we arrived, we rented a car and dutifully drove to the assigned hotel. When we walked into our room, we found a basket of treats and snacks along with a sweet note from Lance's mom. In the note, she welcomed us and gave us recommendations about where to go and what to see while we visited. She also included her phone number. That night, I sat down in the room, took a deep breath, and dialed her number. I wasn't sure if she'd want to speak for just a few minutes or have a more in-depth conversation. I was ready for any response she might have.

As we talked, the minutes turned into an entire hour. Lance's mom, Fin, was a retired university art professor, and she spoke with the gentle kindness of a teacher. She immediately set me at ease with her warmth and compassion. I scribbled quick notes to Ryan to fill him in on the conversation. He was having trouble containing his happy energy. As I talked on the phone, he bounced from one bed to the other, doing flips and jumps that had me worried he'd crack his head open.

The next day, we visited the Norton Simon art museum as recommended by Fin. Then we did some shopping, still unsure of our next steps with Lance's family. As we stood in the check-out line at Banana Republic, I got a call on my cell phone. The caller ID showed the call was coming from Lance.

"You answer it," I said to Ryan, feeling anxiety jangle through my body.

Finding Peace by Connecting the Pieces

"No, you!" he said, shoving the phone back to me, eyes wide.

"No, no, you get it," I said, thinking Lance would rather talk to Ryan.

"No, YOU!" Ryan said, panic sending his voice higher.

Fearing we would lose the call to voice mail, I answered, my hands trembling. Lance sounded friendly and considerably calmer than us. He gave us instructions to meet in the hotel lobby in one hour, then go to lunch together. Ryan and I raced back to the hotel to change and prepare.

Back at the hotel, as I quickly readied, Ryan once again wildly jumped from one bed to the other, hardly able to contain one ounce of his excitement. We only had one chance to make a first impression, and we were on it. I so badly wanted this to go well for Ryan. We decided to time it perfectly so that we would exit the elevator and nonchalantly stroll into the lobby just as Lance walked in. We wanted to look a lot more nonchalant than we felt.

We took the elevator down, found no Lance, then took the elevator back up and started over. We did this about five times until the charade became hilarious and we were cracking up. I was relieved to find some humor in this stressful scenario. In the end, we opted to position ourselves out of sight in the bar adjacent to the lobby. Giggling with nervous laughter, we crouched behind the bar, waiting to spot Lance so that we could make our "casual" entrance.

Several men walked into the hotel lobby, but when Lance arrived, there was no mistaking him. He was tall and physically similar to Ryan, but the real giveaway was his smile. As we walked closer, Ryan's traits jumped right out at me.

He has Ryan's teeth! He's got Ryan's eyebrows!

Then I was shaking the hand of the man who was just as much related to Ryan as I was. It felt humbling and awesome to be standing next to the other half of Ryan's DNA. The best, though, was seeing Ryan meet his biological father.

As we walked around the block to the restaurant, I hung back, marveling at their similar walks. I watched women walk past Lance and then turn to have another look at this very handsome man. The moment was huge, but the conversation, by necessity, started small. Lance asked Ryan about school, and they chatted about their taste in food. Almost immediately after being seated at the restaurant, Ryan and Lance put their hands together to compare, then their feet. It was precious.

Lance recently told me that when we first met, he was thinking, "*Who* are these people, and *why* am I here?" Then, when we sat down at the restaurant and he first looked into Ryan's eyes, he says he saw something so familiar. I think it was then that his questions were answered.

Ryan describes the moment that we sat down as surreal. Here he was sitting at a table with *both* of his parents. He says that he kept looking back and forth at us thinking, "My *mother, AND* ... my *father....*"

I tried to stay in the background of the conversation, offering occasional comments but wanting Ryan to feel that Lance was his. At the end of lunch, Lance invited us to his parents' house for dinner. I was thrilled for Ryan that on this day he would also get to meet his genetic grandparents.

Lance gave us his parents' address—I was relieved to find that the note didn't self-destruct—and we prepared for another stressful but happy meeting. That evening, when we walked in the front door to greet Fin and her husband, Don, we all had big plastered smiles. Clearly everyone shared the anxious excitement of the moment.

Right away, Fin took hold of my hand and said, "Well, you know, dear, we're all a little bit nervous." We all chuckled nervously. As if on cue, Don chimed in, "Who wants a glass of wine?" All the grown-ups quickly exclaimed, "I do!" to more laughter.

After the ice was broken, the evening got easier. When the doorbell rang about half an hour after we arrived, Lance joked, "That better not be Oprah!" We all laughed, and it turned out to be the Chinese food delivery guy. Although it made for a light moment, it revealed Lance's continued preoccupation with Ryan's and my high profile. It clearly bothered him. He did *not* want to be a famous sperm donor.

The evening went well, filled with a nervous giddiness and small talk. Although Lance had called Fin and Don Ryan's grandparents, the relationship didn't quite feel like family that night. Grandmother Fin welcomed us with open arms, but Lance and Don were a little more reserved. I realized that this would move slowly. After all, these people were essentially strangers. I thought it may be a long time before Ryan and I could fully relax and be ourselves around Lance and his family.

On Sunday morning, before we left California, Ryan and I went to Fin and Don's house for breakfast. The smell of French toast filled the air. Ryan and Don sat at the piano together while Don played a beautiful tune. Lance leaned up against the piano, listening. Sunlight streamed through the windows, catching waves of steam from the stove drifting across the room. Fin pranced out of the kitchen wearing an apron, spatula in hand, singing to the music. I couldn't imagine a more perfect scene; I blinked back tears.

I was witness to Ryan's most fervent dreams—and then some—coming true. For me, it felt like possibility. When we arrived, I had no expectations. To be in this Norman Rockwell painting two days later made me think we might be able to redefine our family to include these people. It was a beautiful feeling, and I sensed that the others felt it, too. Many times over that weekend Ryan would look at me, eyes huge, and say, "I know who my donor is."

On the plane ride home, Ryan had a sense of peacefulness about him that I had never seen before. He turned to me and said, "If I never see those people again, I'll be okay, because I know where I come from."

After that trip, Fin and I began talking on the phone every few weeks. She wanted to hear every detail about Ryan's life, both present and past. We talked about everything and discovered so much in common. We both loved travel, history, architecture, and art. They were impressed that Ryan had already traveled the world with me and also appreciated these things. Having so much in common with both Ryan and me certainly made the connecting go much smoother than it might have been otherwise.

It wasn't long before Fin and Don invited Ryan to go to their house for Christmas. Having met them, I felt comfortable sending Ryan alone this time. Fin and Don took great care to know what interested Ryan so they could do things that appealed to him. They clearly wanted this to be a good experience for Ryan.

That Christmas was just Ryan, Lance, and the grandparents. They took him to a car show and attended to his needs and interests. He had a great time.

As we moved into this uncharted territory, Fin and I worked in the background to smooth the way for family gatherings. In our regular calls, we would develop a rough plan that Fin would then mention to Don in a way that convinced him it was his idea. Don was the great organizer. He set the itinerary, chose the activities, and made the reservations.

Fin and I understood that Lance might be struggling to figure out his role with Ryan, so we felt it would be helpful for her and Don to take the lead. For grandparents, it was an easier relationship to slip into. Ryan was their grandson, end of story. My mother had gone to California to meet Fin and Don shortly after our first meeting and brought along many of Ryan's baby photos and videos of his childhood. Later, Fin would tell me that she felt she had to grieve for the 15 missed years of Ryan's life.

Despite my bond with Fin, it wasn't all smooth sailing with Lance and his family. We are very different people. My family is expressive and exuberant. We share our feelings freely and without filters. Hey, we're New Yorkers. In contrast, Lance and his parents were more reserved. Fin said at one point, "We're just not very funny people," ironically one of the funnier things she'd said to me. Fin once described Lance's communication as "telegraph English."

For the first few years, when we received Fin and Don's Christmas cards full of family news, Ryan wasn't in them. That hurt. They had accepted him graciously into their nuclear family, but they weren't willing to introduce him to anyone else. There was something about their secrecy that implied shame. As a mom, it made me angry to see Ryan treated that way. I wondered why they wouldn't want to be proud of Ryan with their own family and friends.

Over time, I have come to see that they just didn't know how to introduce him. Don even said early on, "Well, it's not like we're family, but we could be someday." It was a process, and everyone went at a different speed. For Don, it was slow. It would be years before he and Fin introduced Ryan to their extended family as their grandson or included him in the yearly Christmas newsletter.

Finding Peace by Connecting the Pieces

Lance continued to be tricky to figure out. He could be aloof, then surprise me with his kindness. Knowing about his suspicion of me from the beginning, I treaded lightly, never wanting to cross a boundary. Early on, when he had asked Ryan, "What does your mother want from me?" Ryan had to assure him that this curiosity had nothing to do with his mother. Lance was warm with Ryan—always—and that's what really mattered to me. *Please be kind to my kid* continued to be my mantra. I just kept showing up as my authentic self, with no agenda. I gave myself pep talks about sticking with this process and not getting discouraged by the skepticism from Lance and his dad. I saw my role as clearing a path for Ryan to forge a real relationship with Lance and his parents.

Our next meeting as a big group took place at our house in Colorado. In the few days leading up to the visit, I had a couple of rough email exchanges with Lance. He questioned my motives and wrote some things that really hurt my feelings. It seemed like things could go south.

No, no, I told myself. *We have worked too hard to get to this place.* It had been almost a year since our first meeting in 2005. I saw huge potential for them to become part of our family, and I wanted to keep moving in that direction.

I had to let the emails go. This visit wasn't about me or my hurt feelings. It was about making the trip positive for Ryan, Lance, and his parents. I wanted to make a space for those relationships to develop and deepen. I mentioned nothing about it to Ryan. Whatever Lance said to me needed to be water off a duck's back. I also didn't lose sight of the immediate benefits to me of making this relationship work. The more I learned about Lance and his family, the better information I would have about my own child. After all, this was half of his DNA. I kept that in the front of my mind during rough spots in the relationship.

Despite the ominous start, the visit was a big success. My mom knew how important it was to Ryan to establish relationships with his donor relatives. She had embraced Fin and Don as Ryan's grandparents even before they fully took on those roles. On the last night, everyone from both families gathered for a family dinner at my house. Lance clinked his wine glass and made a toast. He offered the kindest words about me for making the event happen and inviting them into our lives. I could hardly believe what I was hearing. It made my night.

Score! I said to myself.

By showing up and being real, I had chipped away at their misgivings. It gave me the fuel to keep working on the relationships. I felt the possibility that these people could be more than Ryan's family; they might be my family, too.

Expanding Family | 9

As a sperm donor, your agreement with a sperm bank is usually a one-year commitment to come in two or three times a week. Lance donated sperm for five years: during college, graduate school, and his first year of work. Each donation can be separated into anywhere between four and 24 sellable vials, so that's potentially 75 children every week over five years, which equals somewhere around 19,000 potential sellable vials. Even if you take 90% off of that, it's 1,900. And even if you take another 90% off of that, it's still 190. There is no shelf life on the sperm once it's cryogenically frozen; it can last forever. On the Donor Sibling Registry, we have half-siblings who were born decades apart.

Ryan and I knew, with that kind of math, we were bound to discover more half-siblings. After the disappointment of 2003, we kept our excitement in check when a girl named Tiffany contacted us in 2006.

Six months younger than Ryan, Tiffany was born to a single mom who later married. Tiffany's mother had told her that she was a donor baby but discouraged her from researching her donor father or half-siblings. However, Tiffany was bright and curious and had found her way to Ryan on her own. Ryan was thrilled to hear from her, and the 15-year-olds exchanged a flurry of emails. I worried from the beginning, explaining to Tiffany that we would need to bring her mom into the loop as soon as possible.

We told her that Ryan and I would be featured on an upcoming episode of *60 Minutes*. Tiffany latched on to the idea that she and her mom would watch the show together, and it would provide a great way to break the news that Ryan was her half-brother. I wrote a letter to her mom for Tiffany to give to her after the show.

The interview with *60 Minutes* happened after we had found Lance, which made this media appearance more stressful and higher stakes than others before it. Our interviewer, Steve Kroft, said he would have to ask if we had found Ryan's donor.

Lance had made it abundantly clear that he would cut off contact with us if Ryan said publicly that he knew his donor. So, Ryan came up with this answer: "I prefer not to talk about my personal situation with my donor, because it could compromise any future contact I might have with him." Steve asked his question, Ryan answered, and it worked fine.

Being on the *60 Minutes* episode that March felt doubly exciting because of the prospect that Tiffany would tell her mom about Ryan. The plan was that they would call us shortly after the show. Finally, we would connect with one of Ryan's siblings. Not able to contain his happy anticipation on that snowy winter night, Ryan bounced on an exercise ball all the way through the show.

We waited and waited for the call, but it never came. Ryan dealt with another crushing disappointment. A couple of months later, I received a Mother's Day card from Tiffany. She wrote that her mother had reacted badly to her news. "Those people are not your family," her mom had said. She took away Tiffany's phone and shut down her Myspace account, but not before Tiffany posted this message:

For a while I tried searching for my donor. In the beginning I found I had a sibling, then a second! I was both amazed, and emotional *very lol* and yet I couldn't share it w/ anyone, especially my mother, who was against me finding my donor from the beginning. I searched without her knowing— something I have never regretted because I would have never known that there were two people in the world who were a part of me. I would sit w/ her and tried to talk about why I needed to learn about me but she ignored it and would never bring it up. Her feelings are similar to everyone else in my family. Sometimes I feel all alone, like I'm the only one going through this. I know she'll never accept me wanting to know.

My heart broke for Tiffany, whose curiosity was totally natural. We communicated a few times after that before losing touch for good.

The experience renewed my resolve to advocate for openness in the donor community. I was heartened by the connections happening every day on the DSR. The *60 Minutes* episode brought 28,000 visitors to the DSR in March 2006, a huge leap from our usual 8,000. During that month, 538 people matched with half-siblings or donors. The website wasn't working for

Expanding Family

Ryan—yet—but it buoyed my spirits to be facilitating all of these other family connections.

Ryan found other ways to meet donor-conceived kids. We had helped several families through the DSR when they discovered they shared Donor 66. It turned out that four of the Donor 66 moms, with six kids among them, lived in the Denver area. They graciously invited Ryan and me to their barbecues and holiday parties. After our failed half-sibling connections, it lifted us up to be with a group of donor families really embracing and enjoying each other. They made Ryan an honorary "Donor 66 kid."

Then, in February 2007, an alert from the DSR came up on my computer while I was at work. Ryan was doing schoolwork in the office next to mine. We had matched with Anna, a 13-year-old in New York. *Oh, here we go again*, I thought, bracing myself. "Ryan!?" I shouted in my now familiar "we have a sibling" voice.

We shot out an email right away: "Do you have your parents' permission?" We quickly received an email back from Anna's parents, and I allowed myself to hope this one might work out.

As it turned out, Anna had signed up on the DSR with her dad's help. That spoke volumes to me about this man, who probably wasn't 100% comfortable with having his daughter explore her biological relatives when he didn't have that biological connection himself. This was a dad who really loved his daughter; he put her needs before his own.

Very quickly, we all got on the phone together. For Ryan, it was his first conversation with a half-sibling. After seven years, Ryan became the 2,910[th] person to successfully match on the DSR.

Our call with Anna's family was bubbly and chatty and jubilant for everyone. Amazingly, Anna was also born on May 22. As 3-year-old Ryan was blowing out the candles on his Superman cake, Anna was being born. Anna had a new big brother, and Ryan had a new little sister. They were thrilled. Over the next few weeks I talked with Anna's mom several times on the phone.

Ryan's 3rd birthday, 1993, the same day Anna was born

We set up a meeting in New York. *Primetime* on ABC had called to ask if they could update a story they had done four years before on Ryan and the DSR. We thought our joyful meeting with Anna would be a perfect occasion. We would meet Anna in Central Park, cameras capturing the whole thing.

Ryan and I flew to New York City a month later. We were jumping out of our skin with excitement. The morning of the meeting, each family was supposed to have a camera crew with us as we walked toward each other in Central Park. Ryan carried a University of Colorado sweatshirt for Anna. We had set a meeting place, but our two families accidentally bumped into each other walking along the park road, camera crews lagging too far behind.

By the time the camera crews caught up with us, we were already embracing and shedding tears, as the physical resemblance was stunning. I'm not related to Anna, but when I looked at her, I saw parts of my son, and it created a visceral reaction. I just automatically cared about her.

I was overwhelmed with gratitude to Anna's parents that they had been honest with Anna and honored her curiosity, her need to search, and her desire to connect with Ryan.

We spent the first hour asking each other questions, taking pictures, and comparing notes. Ryan and Anna couldn't stop smiling. There was a sense of peace about both of them. We spent the next 48 hours getting to know each other and marveling at the similarities and differences in Ryan and Anna. Anna wore her CU sweatshirt with pride, despite the 75-degree weather.

We told Ryan and Anna that they would define the relationship and there was no pressure for it to look a certain way. We stayed in touch with Anna's family by email and phone. We made plans to celebrate Ryan's 18th and Anna's 15th birthday together the next year.

Anna and her family were the first people we told when we got another match in 2008. Ryan and I had appeared on *Oprah* again, producing another big surge of new members on our website. One of those was a mom of two donor-conceived daughters in Massachusetts. The mom, who had the full support of her husband and a couple of curious teen girls, sent me an email about "that lady and her son on *Oprah*," not realizing I was that lady and Ryan was her daughters' half-brother. Again, Ryan and I flew east to meet his new sisters, Natalie and Kristina, and their mom, all of whom were invited to celebrate Anna's 15th and Ryan's 18th birthday with us at Anna's home.

Ryan and Anna were pros. They led the way and made it easy for Natalie and Kristina, setting the pace and tone for how the four teens would get to know each other and begin to establish sibling bonds. They played games and hung out, like typical teens. Even though we began as strangers, I immediately cared about Natalie and Kristina the same way I did about Anna. These children who are one-half Lance share certain characteristics, temperament, physical attributes, and medical issues. We moms were raising the same donor's kids, so it felt as though we were travelling through similar territory. It created a special bond among us.

I kept Lance informed about Ryan's sibling matches but continued to honor his request for privacy. We shared relevant information about his health history with the siblings and answered their questions, but we never revealed his identity. Lance's position stayed the same for many years, and we honored that. But I didn't want to lie about it, and I didn't want Ryan to lie about it. So, we would tell the half-siblings, "We know who he is, but we can't tell you who he is. We'll answer any questions you have about him. If there's a question we can't answer, we're happy to go ask Lance or his parents." We showed photos, although not online.

The whole idea that Ryan was allowed to know Lance but the other kids weren't never sat well with me. Ryan's half-siblings are no less Lance's children than Ryan is. Struggling with this tension between secrecy and privacy was my own biggest battle during that time. I disliked secrecy, but I wanted to respect privacy. Trying to discern the boundary between the two was tricky. With so much at stake, I needed to walk the line carefully. At one time, I even consulted a therapist about it. If Lance perceived that I had violated his request for privacy, it would mean my son losing his biological dad. At the same time, I felt a responsibility to Ryan's half-siblings and their right to know about their genetic father. I also felt responsible as the leader of the DSR, which tries to foster transparency in donor family relationships.

I never discussed any of my concerns with Lance. We didn't have an easy relationship like that. I just tried my hardest to handle things in the best way possible for everyone.

To my surprise, Lance and his parents agreed to meet Anna and her parents when they came to Ryan's University of Colorado graduation and party. It was a wonderful experience for everyone and we even got to snap photos. It was 2008. For Lance, and for sperm donors everywhere, we were well into the sunset hours of donor anonymity.

Anna and Ryan, 2018

Empty Nest and the DSR | 10

By 2008, Ryan knew he had six half-sisters, three he had been able to meet and three he hadn't. None of them were "like him," in the way he had hoped when he was little. Certainly, they are all very bright, but neither Lance nor any of the half-siblings had tested as profoundly gifted like Ryan. Ryan discovered that meeting his half-siblings gave him a sense of belonging in another way. He could look into their faces and see a bit of himself. He could talk to them about the experience of being a donor-conceived kid. Meeting his half-sisters satisfied that hunger in him to find his genetic family. He certainly felt that he'd accomplished what he set out to do, although he occasionally wondered, "Why only girls?"

We went through another dry spell with siblings, and Ryan turned his focus to graduate school. At 18, he was finishing up his undergraduate work in aerospace engineering at the University of Colorado and looking for an engineering graduate program. It was between Duke University and the University of Southern California.

As we did with Lance's identity, we made a chart with a line down the middle: Duke on one side, USC on the other. At the top of the USC side were Fin and Don. In Pasadena, his grandparents would be able to see him regularly. I hoped Ryan would choose that option. Not only was it closer to home, but I would have peace of mind knowing that family was nearby.

In the end, that's what Ryan chose. In August, we packed up and drove out to Pasadena to move Ryan into his apartment, just a bike ride away from his grandparents. The night before I left L.A., we stayed at Fin and Don's house. Fin sat with me on the guest-room bed, holding my hand and consoling me as tears streamed down my face. By now, she and Don felt like family. I was so relieved that they would be there for Ryan, but it didn't make leaving him easy. The next day when Ryan dropped me at the airport, I stayed composed until he pulled away. Then I cried all the way through security, while I sat at my gate, and during the entire plane ride home.

Ryan and I were close, even for a single mom and only son. His unique childhood, all the tough decisions we had made together, the hard times in school, and the huge moments with his donor family forged an extremely strong bond. That separation was brutal.

I'd read enough about empty nesters to know that everything I was going through was normal—normal, but excruciating. I think that other only-parents of a single child might be able to relate: Making a healthy separation from your adult child can be a lot harder than you thought it might be. At times I found myself pulling away too far, wanting to make sure I gave him enough space to live his own life. We struggled to disentangle our lives from each other.

But I knew that to be a good parent, I needed to give him both roots and wings. I had worked hard on the roots. He had me and my extended family, Lance and his parents, his half-siblings, and our group of fellow donor families. This was his time to grow wings. He'd had increasing independence through his teens, and he'd learned so much about the world through our travels. Now he needed to do it on his own. It was really tough for both of us.

I cried for a month and wondered if I could ever get myself to stop. Eventually, I woke up one morning, went for a hike, and didn't cry. Of course, I still cried occasionally, but it was no longer how I started every day. I found solace in knowing that Ryan went to Fin and Don's regularly for dinner and that they were getting to know each other in a different, more normal way.

During the year Ryan attended USC, we chatted for a good part of each day over instant messenger. Even if we weren't chatting, we always had the chat box open, which was important to both of us. I wanted him to know that I was there for him as he maneuvered through this transition into adult life.

As I adjusted to an empty house and a routine without Ryan, I also began a new working life. The Donor Sibling Registry had for many years demanded a significant amount of my time. By 2005, it was a full-time job on top of my other full-time jobs that actually paid the bills. Over the years, I had worked in accounting and business management and also owned a restaurant. I always had multiple plates spinning.

When I wrote the last check for Ryan's graduate school in October 2009, a couple of months after saying goodbye to Ryan, it felt like a tremendous accomplishment. I had paid for all of his education. *Done!* I sang to myself. I quit my day job and gave myself the luxury of focusing exclusively on the DSR.

After our first appearance on *Oprah*, the DSR had begun to feel like Ryan's academic career—a speeding car dragging me behind it. I never anticipated how much it would grow. It kept expanding, despite what I had the capability to handle.

When we incorporated as a non-profit in 2003, I couldn't imagine the role that I would play in the coming years. The lawyer I hired to file the 501(c)3 papers wrote that I would be speaking at conferences, writing papers, and making more media appearances. At the time, I found her predictions utterly ridiculous. *Who am I to be speaking? I'm just a mom of a donor kid.*

"Okay, if that's what you need to put in your articles of incorporation," I told her. Back then, I felt zero empowerment to do anything beyond start a website for people in my same situation. It was only because of a friend's advice that I decided to make the DSR a non-profit. I certainly didn't think of myself as an expert in anything.

For the first five years of the DSR, I worked for free, and we limped along on a few donations. I was shocked when Stu, a former sperm donor in England excited by the DSR's potential to change the donor family landscape with a comprehensive database matching system, sent $1,000 to help get the DSR website off the ground. Mostly, though, I used my own money to build the site. My business strategy was simply to beg people for donations. After *Oprah*, when traffic to our site got crazy, family and friends hit me over the head, saying that I needed to start charging a membership fee.

The move scared me. On the internet, it's so tough to begin charging for something people have been getting for free. But the bigger we got, the more money it took to run the site. We were going to have to collect fees or go bust.

In 2005, I started charging $25 for a year of membership. In some ways, my fears were realized, because all hell broke loose. People called me greedy. Some said, "How dare you take advantage of donor-conceived people and their curiosity?" It hurt me, because I had worked so long and hard on this site, and I had done it out of a genuine desire to help people.

I think people didn't understand the reality of how the website runs. Just because it's a non-profit doesn't mean we don't have bills. We have typical business expenses, including the cost of a web developer as well as my own time. The bottom line was that we weren't getting enough donations to cover our costs. To this day, the DSR runs primarily on the membership fees. We receive a few small donations here and there, but we have no major funders, and I'm proud to say we are a very healthy 501(c)3. As we rebuild the front and back ends of the DSR website in 2020, costs will likely reach $200,000. Without the membership fees, the 2003 back-end code would have become obsolete and unworkable, and the DSR would have sadly come to an end.

I was never sure how my role or the organization itself would evolve, but I have always felt certain of my commitment to it. So many people asked me after we found Lance whether we would close the site. "Mission accomplished, right?" they said. That possibility never entered my mind. The DSR was never just about Ryan; it was about all donor kids and families. And having seen what it meant to Ryan to meet Lance, it made me even more dedicated to helping other families make these types of connections. I wanted others to be able to have the same opportunities that Ryan had to explore his donor family. On top of all that, Ryan still had siblings to find. Indeed, looking at the math, he will likely always have more siblings to find. Each day for the rest of his life holds the possibility of a new half-sibling coming along. That's true for all donor-conceived people.

My dedication to the DSR and commitment to Ryan's relationship with his donor family have given me a wealth of experience. While I didn't see it coming back in 2003, the organization and my role in it have evolved just as my lawyer predicted. I've been speaking publicly about the DSR and donor conception for years, and, after all this time, I feel comfortable calling myself an expert.

In 2020, the DSR is hopping. Of our 75,000 members, we have matched around 20,000 of them. We make two or three matches every single day. I spend 60 and sometimes 80 hours a week running the organization. When a call comes in for our media, research, counseling, or membership departments, my answer is, "That's me!" I also do the business management side, the accounting, and filings for a charity.

At first just a place for sperm donor families to connect, the DSR soon welcomed egg donor families. Embryo families came next. Once people realized that they had the right to be curious, search for, and find their own or their child's genetic relatives, the DSR became their next stop.

The bulk of what I do every day—and what keeps me going—is helping people. I take calls from people at all different stages of the process: from families at the very beginning of this journey to donor-conceived adults who have just found out, to parents who are about to tell the truth to their adult children, to donors who just found out that they have dozens of donor offspring.

While each situation is unique, donor stories usually follow the same emotional trajectory. Not only have I been through so much of it within our own family, I've also helped so many others with similar stories. At this point, I'm very clear regarding what to say in order to provide the most help. I also listen, because people want to know they're heard and they're not alone. It's comforting for those who call the DSR to know that many have walked this path before them ... and they've all survived. It's important for them to know that they're part of a large community. I lay that out right off the bat, and I can almost hear the sigh of relief on the phone.

If I'm talking to parents, the most common thing I hear is, "My kids just found out that we haven't told them the truth, and they're really angry. What do I do?" I also talk to parents who have young children whom they haven't told but want to. "How do I tell my child?" "How do I then support their curiosities?"

I hear from too many parents who have told their children about the donor conception but don't honor their children's curiosity about their donor and half-siblings. I usually say, "It's great that you've told them, but what's more important is that your child feels they have the right to be curious about, search for, and connect with their genetic family." It's important for parents to understand that it is an innate human desire to want to know where we come from, and *who* we come from. And it's extremely important for donor offspring to know that their parents support them as they search for their ancestry, medical history, and close genetic relatives. Children need to know that this innate curiosity is in no way a betrayal of the parents who raised them.

Sometimes, I hear parents say that they're waiting for their children to be old enough to show curiosity about their half-siblings before allowing contact. I find this odd, as we don't wait for our children to express curiosity about their grandparents or aunts and uncles before introducing them, people who are also anywhere from 15%-30% genetically related to our children. We know that half-sibling relationships can be both enriching and important to a donor child as they grow up. Most children grow up knowing all their relatives, so why exclude half-siblings or even their other biological parent from a child's life, if those relationships are available?

If parents are uncomfortable, we talk about it. We discuss what it might mean for their children to find genetic relatives and what that would look like. It's important for parents to know that connecting with new genetic relatives will not take away from the current family system but might even add to it—that these new connections could be enriching for everyone.

I also talk to many donor-conceived people who have just found out the truth about their conception, quite often these days from DNA testing. Ryan was the first donor-conceived person to find his donor via DNA testing, but he opened a door for thousands of others. I often hear, "What does this mean? Who am I? What is this new family to me? Why did my parents lie?" They're upset, but sometimes also happy and excited and even relieved. At the beginning, there can be a lot of confusion and stress, and I help them navigate through whatever bundle of emotions they're dealing with.

Half-sibling and donor connections can be profound. Besides sharing medical information, many parents of donor kids create wonderful half-sibling communities. Often, donors incorporate their donor children into their existing families, as the children that the donor is raising are half-siblings to the children created with the donor's sperm. Donor offspring sometimes find a whole new family support system. Also, many parents of donors are thrilled to meet their child's donor-conceived children and welcome them as grandchildren.

However, it doesn't always work that way. Just because you're genetically related to someone doesn't guarantee that you'll like them. We know that already. Just look around your own dinner table on Thanksgiving: Do you want to hang out with everyone at that table? Probably not, but that doesn't make those people any less related to you.

With donor families, just like any other family, it's complicated.

The Roaring Twenties | 11

The subject line of the email was familiar: "Donor 1058?" I opened it with less trepidation than I had in the past, but I still held my breath. It was August 2016, and *The New York Times* had just run an article about me, Ryan, and the Donor Sibling Registry. A mom was writing to ask if my actual donor number was 1058.

I replied, and within minutes we were talking on the phone. This mom had a son, younger than Ryan by 18 months, from the same donor. He didn't know he was donor-conceived, but she and his dad planned to tell him soon. We had the typical talk that I offer to donor parents facing this major revelation, but with extra excitement for what it would mean for Ryan: his first brother.

Charlie and his mom stopped in San Francisco a few months later and met Ryan for lunch. I was there too, albeit just a face on a FaceTime screen. It was so cool to "meet" Charlie's mom, with whom I'd struck up a friendship, and to see what characteristics Ryan shared with Charlie and Charlie shared with Lance. Ryan and Charlie moved slowly, both adults busy with their own careers and both considerate of the fact that not everyone in Charlie's family was on board with Charlie's new relative. Having a non-biological parent not thrilled about their kid's donor family connections is something that's all too common in the donor family world and, unfortunately, something also familiar to us personally.

After a painfully slow start, a rush of half-siblings has come forward in recent years. Lance was promised no more than 10 kids by California Cryobank. In early 2020, 20 of Lance's donor-conceived children have connected: 17 girls and three boys. I laugh about it, and it sounds crazy even to me, but it's also so normal. We have sibling groups much bigger than that on the DSR. Many groups are now more than 100, all the way up to 200.

I've talked to many moms of donor-conceived people who feel similar to me in that there is some kind of comfort felt, knowing that when we're no longer around, our kids will have all these other family members to know for the rest of their lives. This is especially true for those of us with only children.

These days, most adult donor-conceived people are coming to the DSR after finding out that they're donor-conceived via DNA websites. Most of Ryan's half-siblings to come along in recent years—the ones in their 20s—had no idea that their dad wasn't also their biological father until they received results from Ancestry or 23andMe. They did the test out of curiosity about their ancestry, not because they were looking for half-siblings.

When Lance's newest donor offspring received their results from the commercial DNA testing sites, they immediately had access to their close relatives. These people got a link to a page with a list of half-siblings they'd never heard of. I can only imagine how shocking and confusing that must have been for them, as, up until that point, they believed that their dad was their biological father.

Donor siblings already registered on those sites receive an email about a new close relative. They then reach out and gently let the new sibling know about how exactly they're related, the other family connections, and the DSR. This is happening more and more, not just with Ryan's half-siblings, but with all donor-conceived people. Obviously, it's key to have older donor siblings populating these DNA sites in order to locate matches and connect them to each other and to the DSR, where others may be waiting. For families with young children who are not yet comfortable testing their children's DNA, connecting on the DSR is still the most popular way to find half-siblings and donors.

In 2018, the Donor 1058 kids realized that none of them were registered at Ancestry.com, so Anna volunteered to spit in the tube and get on that site. She instantly located their half-sister Amanda, who had been all alone on Ancestry for six weeks. Amanda had always suspected that she was adopted or perhaps the result of an affair, so she felt relieved to learn that she was actually donor-conceived. Since then, Anna and Amanda have matched with another half-sibling on Ancestry. It's important to be on both 23andMe and Ancestry, as well as on the DSR, as you could have relatives waiting on any of these sites.

I thought that the rising popularity of these DNA sites might make the DSR obsolete, and I was okay with that. It seemed like a natural progression. But it's been quite the opposite. When people find out they're donor-conceived, they come to us to connect with donor siblings and find education and support. For many years we sent people to DNA testing sites to confirm relatedness, but now it's a two-way highway, as many now also come to the DSR from the DNA testing sites.

It's an understandably tumultuous time when kids and young adults discover that they don't come from where they thought they did. I like to think the DSR helps them process the news, feel less alone, and learn how to cope with their new idea of family.

It doesn't always come as a total shock to people, however. Sometimes, they do the DNA testing because of a gut feeling they always had. Some of Ryan's half-siblings had no idea, some were told but then never spoken to about it again, and a few just knew something was off. Several, like Amanda, wondered if their mom maybe had an affair, or if they were adopted. These kids asked their parents over and over, "Was I adopted?" When their parents denied it, they internalized that denial, and it made them doubt their gut feelings. They learned not to trust themselves. When they later learned the truth, it was a huge sense of relief and validation. They could finally tell themselves, "I'm not crazy."

Then, of course, comes the anger and the hurt. Some feel like they were gaslighted. "I gave my parents all these opportunities to tell me the truth and they didn't." There is a whole array of emotions, and everybody has a slightly different process for working through it. A lot of how easy or difficult the discovery process becomes is based on how stable the parent-child relationship is. When all is said and done, though, I believe that the only way forward is through finding forgiveness.

When donors do DNA testing, there's a chance they'll connect with the children conceived from their donations. Many donors call me with questions after seeing their offspring pop up on these DNA sites. I tell them to join the DSR and read the testimonials, the advice, and the research. Other donors, like Lance, don't submit their DNA but are found through other relatives who do. When Ryan tested his DNA, the database was little more than 20,000 people. Now DNA databases are around 30 million, so finding anyone, directly or indirectly, has become relatively easy.

When someone becomes a member of the DSR, they can test the waters, because everyone is anonymous to each other. We don't share contact information unless our members choose to share it. Members can provide medical information, photos, and messages, all while remaining private, if that's how they want to join at the beginning. When and if they're ready, they can take steps to meet or talk with their donor kids.

Many donors do end up providing their email addresses and phone numbers. Some people connect, and the next day they're meeting for coffee. Other people, just by their nature or because of distance, take things more slowly. The DSR is a vehicle they can use to go as slow or fast as they want. There's no right or wrong way to do it.

I try to educate donors about what these connections mean and what they don't mean. Donor-conceived people are not on the DSR looking for money or for a mom or dad. They just want to know more about themselves and their own identity, ancestry, and medical history. I believe that you can't fully know who you are until you know where and who you come from. We're all a unique blend of nature and nurture: the blueprint we're born with along with our families, communities, and life experiences. For me, seeing the similarities in our own donor family and in thousands of other families has made the scales tip toward nature—our DNA—playing a larger role in determining our destinies.

One donor reported this to us about California Cryobank: "They were quite strong in their position that I should NOT register on the DSR." The sperm banks continue to put fear in donors that these genetic children will disrupt their lives. In my experience, that's never the case. I see my job as setting the record straight on that front. Once donors understand what donor-conceived people are looking for, I find they are much more comfortable moving forward. Usually, the sperm banks' main concern is their own liability. The more that people connect, the more the sperm banks' lies and inconsistencies are uncovered. False claims of limiting the number of kids born to any one donor or the sperm bank's untrue promises of both updating and sharing of medical information have only become known since the families started connecting and sharing information on the DSR.

In the summer of 2018, after an eight-year sibling dry spell for Ryan followed by a quick jump from 10 to 16 confirmed half-siblings, I created an Excel spreadsheet to keep track of the kids' names, locations, and birth dates. Soon after that, I made a Facebook group for the offspring and families of Donor 1058. Some of us were on the DSR, others on Ancestry or 23andMe, so we needed a platform where we could all get to know each other, share photos, and exchange medical information. I thought it would be especially helpful for the newer siblings to have a soft landing pad, a place where they could watch from the sidelines if they weren't quite ready to jump in and explore new relationships.

The Donor 1058 kids share many things: Sometimes it's their temperament or the way they think, and sometimes it's the way they walk, or their fabulous hair. Several are quite artistic. More than a few have struggled with OCD, anxiety, and depression. They're also really empathetic and very socially conscious. Each has at least a few things in common with every other sibling. They are spread from coast to coast, in Puerto Rico, and one was raised in France. There are twins, singletons, and sisters, coming from mostly heterosexual parents who also struggled with male infertility.

I try to hang back on the Facebook page. Still, all the siblings know this is my life, as my role for so long has been clearing a path for all donor families to create relationships. I'm not just any mom, I'm Wendy of the DSR, and their half-brother is Ryan of the DSR. I've been told that a couple of the half-siblings have joked with each other that they joined the royalty of donor families.

Some siblings ask health questions, some announce or share big events in their lives. The group helps these people understand that they're not alone on their journey, that there are others walking side by side down the same path also trying to make sense of their expanding family and incorporating this new knowledge into their identities.

The parents of the donor siblings are welcome to join the 1058 group as well. Some moms have joined, but not one of the dads. That speaks to the dynamics of these newer sibling families, who kept their kids in the dark for a reason. Usually, that reason is the non-biological parent, and for 1058 families, this has always been the dad. The family sometimes fears hurting the dad, or worries that the family system will be negatively affected or maybe even collapse. The dad may also feel threatened or betrayed by their child's interest to know the once invisible rest of their genetic family and roots.

Lance has also joined the Facebook group. Becoming more open was a slow evolution for him. Early on, with each new half-sibling, he seemed ambiguous, worried, sometimes even skeptical, but also curious. When

Ryan and I got together with Lance, we would tell him about the half-siblings, but it always felt like they existed in a separate world.

Creating the Facebook group seemed like a tipping point for him. It helped that these donor-conceived kids were adults now. Most of them have dads. They don't want anything from Lance. Whatever he may have been worried about didn't happen. Lance participates on the page just as much or as little as everybody else. He seems truly interested in everyone's well-being, and he offers up medical and ancestral information. The relief for me is huge, because I'm no longer walking that slippery ridge between secrecy and privacy. I'm not the gatekeeper anymore, and that feels great.

When we hit 20 siblings, I sent Lance a message: "Just checking in, are you okay?" He seems very comfortable with it at this point, excited and happy every time a new sibling comes along. I think he now knows that he gets to define these relationships for himself, and that his boundaries will always be respected.

With the popularity of DNA testing sites, donors are realizing there is little chance they can remain anonymous, despite what the sperm banks may have promised. As we discovered in our search for Lance, even a distant relative in the DNA database can link a child to his donor. For donor-conceived people, when they connect on DNA websites with several or many half-siblings but have thought all along that they had a biological connection to both of their parents, their worlds can feel like they're turning upside down. Finding Ryan's donor and half-siblings has certainly been way more complicated than we ever imagined. When you have families where there's been infertility, secrecy, and shame, it can make the connecting quite challenging at times. In that way, our group is no different from any other on or off the DSR.

Thanks for the Kid | 12

I had always thought that the only thing I wanted from Lance was his kindness to my son. Shortly after we met and Lance's warm treatment of Ryan allayed my fears, I realized that I wanted one more thing—for me. I wanted to hear Lance say, "You did a good job."

I had thrown my heart and soul, sweat and tears into being Ryan's only parent. Of course, it was a joy to be his mom, but it was also wildly challenging, as all parents know. Getting him out of an abusive home and making it on our own, negotiating crazy academic decisions, and helping him search for his biological father were all things I doubted I could do. But we did them, and Ryan turned out to be a wonderful human being.

I sensed Lance's pride in having helped create this wonderkid who studied aerospace engineering at age 14 and who ended up with the exact same master's degree. Still, I hoped that Lance would more directly acknowledge my role as Ryan's parent. He didn't—not in the beginning.

Although I didn't hear those words from Lance, I heard them all the time from Fin. Lance's mom made it clear that I had earned her seal of approval in my parenting of Ryan. She was so proud of him and honored to be his grandma.

Fin's affection for Ryan made me love her even more. I'm not sure how I would have navigated those early days with Lance without Fin's support. She and I were like partners in crime. Over long, chatty phone calls, we shared information about our families and plotted our next get-togethers. She was our champion, encouraging and supporting both Ryan and me every step of the way. Lance and Don eventually came around, and I know they care about both of us, but Fin was in our corner from the beginning. It helped immeasurably to have her by my side.

Fin sent Ryan a manila envelope of clippings every month when he was in college. They contained hundreds of newspaper and magazine articles and even a few cartoons that struck her funny bone. The articles covered science, nutrition, genetics, aerospace, and robotics—basically anything she thought might be of interest. Those mailings were her way of letting Ryan know that he was often in her thoughts.

In 2018, Fin went to Dallas to visit Lance's brother, and she collapsed in a restaurant. A couple of days later, on October 11, she died. I miss her dearly.

Ryan was in Thailand, so he had to miss Fin's memorial service. I attended with Ryan's new half-sister Amanda and the mom of another half-sibling. I did ask permission to bring them, as neither of these women had met Lance or Don before. It was heartbreaking to think that they would never get to know Fin as the wonderful grandmother she was. As we sat together at the celebration of life, they supported me in my grief and I supported them in their first-time donor family meetings. I was honored to be the first person that Lance asked to speak, which was an acknowledgement of the bond that Fin and I had created together. It was an emotional day.

I have always felt that Lance offered Ryan as a gift to his parents, so that they could enjoy grandparenthood. And Fin surely did enjoy being a grandma. Her loss hit me really hard; I still struggle with that hole in my life. But she's left the family in a good place. Ryan and Lance have a relationship that I no longer need to facilitate or worry about, and I finally did get that validation from Lance that I craved for years.

Ryan's work trajectory after grad school had taken him from NASA's Jet Propulsion Laboratory in Pasadena to working for a Colorado company on its space shuttle program. Then in 2014, he moved on to Apple and subsequently landed at Google's life sciences company Verily in San Francisco, where Lance also lived.

In 2016, I went to visit Ryan in San Francisco. Lance suggested we all meet for happy hour at a bar downtown. Ryan and I arrived to a packed house and spotted Lance at a distance. We began snaking our way through the crowd, and as we got close, I heard Lance say to his friend, "Check it out. See that kid? He's my son." He said it with pride in his voice. When we joined them, Lance introduced Ryan as his son and told a bit about his accomplishments. The friend said, "Wow, you must be really proud of him." Lance shook his head. "Not me, it's all her," he said, pointing at me. "She's his mother, and she did it all. I had nothing to do with it." While only half true, it was a kind and generous comment, and the words I had been waiting to hear for more than 10 years

More recently, Ryan and I took a trip to Hong Kong together for a DSR speaking engagement, and I stayed at Lance's house before we left. The next day, I wrote him a quick thank-you email for letting me use his guest room. Lance wrote back just one line: "Thanks for the kid." Lance doesn't gush, so from him, those words meant the world to me. In the years I waited for some acknowledgment from Lance, I never felt any anger or resentment about it. I was working with so many donor families that I had a well of experience to pull from. I knew that every family's path is different, and sometimes patience is needed.

I knew where I wanted us to go, that I wanted Ryan to be able to forge a bond with his biological family. The obstacles didn't deter me. I guess that's pretty engrained in *my* DNA. When I'm driving the train, you better believe it will leave the station—on time. My determined personality is perhaps the reason that Ryan had been the only one of Lance's donor-conceived kids who has had a real relationship with him. Several other donor children and their families have met Lance and his parents over the years, but neither side pursued anything more. For some of the donor recipient parents and kids, maybe it was just less important to them or maybe they didn't know how to do it. Or, perhaps they were concerned for the dad and their own family's stability and privacy.

13 | *Portland*

In late 2019, one of Ryan's half-sisters invited all of her half-siblings to her wedding. I had gotten to know this particular half-sister a little bit, so I was also invited to attend. To me, this was an opportunity. I rented a gorgeous large house in a beautiful wooded section of Portland, invited the half-siblings and Lance (who wasn't invited to the wedding as it might be too distracting), and hoped for the best. It was an amazing and profound experience, and one I'll never forget: Seven half-siblings and Lance finally had the opportunity to get to know one another.

Ryan and five of his half-siblings, in Portland in 2019

There was a lot of laughter and even some tears as the 1058 group shared their life experiences and family stories honestly and with great trust, knowing they were in the company of empathetic and supportive "family." More than one of the stories ended with "It's complicated."

Lance was open, inquiring, interested, supportive, and friendly, with a smile plastered on his face, obviously very happy to be included in the gathering. One night at dinner, on the exact one-year anniversary of Lance's mother's death, he shared the eulogy that he had read at her service. As I looked around the table, each sibling was raising their napkin to wipe tears and then, starting with Natalie, there came several hugs from the group. My heart broke for Lance and his loss, and also for his mother, Fin, for having to miss out on this magical event. Lance did invite to dinner the night before some family who happened to live in Portland. Two of Fin's sisters along with a couple of cousins got to join in the festivities and witness first-hand what it's like to have a gathering of very closely related strangers.

Over the course of the weekend, the siblings shared their life stories and their struggles with depression and anxiety. Some shared the difficulties of finding out about being donor-conceived via a DNA test, and some shared about other family members who were not supportive or who refused to discuss these new donor family relations. On the last evening together, a wild karaoke night out seemed to solidify the sibling connections. The sisters did a Spice Girls song, Ryan and Charlie performed an R&B duet, and, finally, they all joined in for the Pokémon theme song.

These young adults and Lance walked through the colorful stained-glass front door of the Portland home as virtual strangers into an unknown experience with a sense of courage, openness, excitement, and vulnerability. They were "sisters from the same mister" and "brothers from another mother." They left both as friends and family, talking about whose wedding would come next so that they could meet up again.

That weekend, Lance and I took a couple of long walks together, around the city and through our wooded neighborhood, the first time that we had ever spent one-on-one time talking in this way. It was meaningful. I feel like we solidified our undefinable relationship, finally, after almost 15 years. We both love Ryan, and having that in common binds us together for life.

Webster's dictionary describes a pivotal moment: *"Pivotal moments are big moments and little moments of clarity that provide us with new perspectives and opportunities to change our lives."* For me, this weekend was pivotal, as it expanded the way I see the donor family experience and will affect the way I approach and consult with donor families in the future. I was able to witness what's possible when love is put before fear. Even though I am not related to any of the half-siblings or Lance, I care about all of them and their happiness, as they all share in something so dear to me, my son.

Ryan's half-sister Jami shared some of her feelings about the Portland weekend with me:

I walked out of the weekend after meeting all of my half-siblings and my donor on cloud 9. I had been working in therapy in the weeks leading up to the gathering. What if I didn't like someone? What if they offended me, or we didn't agree on something? This was my "what if" brain working in overdrive ... it was an exciting yet scary weekend to be walking into, and I really just wanted the best for everyone involved. My fears melted immediately after meeting everyone. I felt love in the room. We were all curious, maybe a little reserved, but respecting each other, our journeys, and our possible permanent places in each other's lives moving forward. I noticed myself thinking, "I love her" about one of my half-sisters not even two hours after knowing her. The thought took me back a bit, but I told myself it's okay to love these people. Everyone that came to the half-siblings gathering that weekend wanted to know their half-siblings, and that leaves a chance of loving your half-siblings. I felt like I could be myself, which is huge because I can be silly and goofy, loud and obnoxious. I felt the same love being given back to me. None of my fears or anxieties that I had worked out in therapy came to fruition. I couldn't have asked for a better weekend, and I truly feel so blessed that everyone brought their authentic selves to the table for us to learn about and love.

Sam, who had only found out via a DNA test earlier in the year that the dad who raised her wasn't her biological father, shared her thoughts with Lance and me before the weekend had even ended:

I sought out clarification by driving across the country to visit my half-siblings and biological father at a reunion in Portland, Oregon. I lost my self in the faces of each new relative I met. Searching for resemblance in the shape of our eyes, in the movements of our bodies, in the color of our skin tones. I discovered that the anxiety and depression I had struggled with all my life was a struggle we shared. And I discovered that I couldn't exactly understand what it meant to be related by blood, but I decided it did mean something.

This experience has expanded my worldview. It has forced me to delve into concepts I had never fathomed before. How does one define family? How does one define a stranger? How do we decide what strangers become family, and how do we decide what family would be better off as strangers? Who do we allow into our lives, and how much of ourselves do we let them know? What inherent values lie in titles like mother, father, sibling? And who do these titles belong to? These definitions and boundaries are in no way clear or cemented, and I will redefine and renegotiate them until the day I die.

On the last day, as I was driving the "1058-mobile" van that I had rented for the weekend, Lance sat beside me as the navigator, and Ryan and his half-sister Natalie sat in the back. Ryan joked, "I just have to say ... that I never would have imagined that I'd be sitting in the back seat of a van beside my *sister* with my *two parents* up front!" We all laughed, and Lance playfully told the siblings in the back seat to behave themselves.

One takeaway for me in watching these different interactions is that relationships take a ton of work. For Ryan, it was important to know Lance and for Lance to know him, so I did the heavy lifting to get the ball rolling. Donor family relationships require effort but also courage because you're putting yourself out into the great unknown. They also take exposing a little of your own vulnerability and being willing to face head-on some uncomfortable feelings. I understand and witnessed first-hand that weekend that sometimes the emotional bandwidth is just not there, especially when family support and encouragement are missing. But for the half-siblings who showed up and embraced each other, I have a feeling that the beginnings of some wonderful connections were established—although only time will tell.

14 | *Continuing to Redefine Family*

When we started the DSR, Ryan and I held hands and jumped off the cliff together. We didn't know who we would find or who would find us, but we were able to take each step—and make each leap—because we had each other's hand.

I have encountered so many donor families who act out of fear, not love. They would rather perpetuate a lie than do the work of embracing and sharing the truth. Our children, however, deserve truth and respect. They have a right know and to be known by their genetic relatives. They have a right to their origin story. But telling is only the first step, as donor-conceived people also deserve to have any curiosities about their ancestry, medical history, and close genetic relatives honored. This has been my philosophy and the guiding principle for the DSR. I regularly counsel with people who are just about to tell and with those who have just told, so I know that telling can be scary. But it can also be a healing experience for the family—when parents are prepared to put the feelings of their child ahead of their own fears or shame. The shame of infertility can be healed and not passed along to the child as the shame of donor conception. The burden of this secret is not for the parents to carry; this truth is owed to the child.

Ryan's two half-sisters, the ones we first connected with after *Oprah* in 2003, have still not been told the truth. They are now in their mid-20s, and it's only a matter of time before they too spit into a tube and receive some shocking news: Not only are they donor-conceived, but their mother has known about Ryan and the other half-siblings over the years. I have kept her in the loop, encouraging her each time I've contacted her to tell her daughters.

One of Ryan's half-sisters explains:

I found out at age 28 through AncestryDNA, which I signed up for because I had suspected my dad wasn't my biological father my entire life. I wish so badly that my parents had just told me as a child, because growing up I was so different from them and my siblings but I didn't have any way of explaining why. It made me feel like an outsider in my own family, and I felt like I was crazy. Having this information from an early age could have drastically improved my quality of life growing up. This is an important truth of our existence. The shame or discomfort you may feel about telling your child is nothing compared to the gaslighting and distress we experience from being lied to our whole lives.

And from another half-sister:

My mother told me at age 18 very abruptly. After the initial first discussion, it was never brought up again. I felt alone, angry, sad, and confused. I had no one to talk to about what I was going through. I have spent the past five years of my life trying to process those emotions and thoughts alone, with no follow-up from either of my parents. I was scared to ask questions. I didn't know where to start or what to ask. Not only is bringing the truth to life important, but also being there for your child after they know. There will never be a "perfect" or "right" time to tell your children. I wish that someone had chosen to be honest with me when I was younger because we could have avoided these past five years of intense emotions and confusion for me.

We've seen how making contact via the DSR can greatly differ from connecting via DNA testing sites with relatives who might be shocked by their new genetic connections. Trying to establish new relationships via DNA with people who may not be prepared for this type of new-relative connection can be a very different experience than making deliberate mutual consent contact on the DSR. While the level of desired contact may vary, by making yourself available to be found on the DSR, you can be assured that any results you receive come with the certainty and confirmation that the person you're connecting with will not be shocked by the news that they are donor-conceived. Indeed, chances are that they'll be thrilled to have made the connection. In contrast, connecting via DNA can be so shocking that some are not even prepared to reply to messages from their new-found relatives on the DNA websites. For those waiting for a reply that never comes, this can be difficult.

The nature of families is always evolving, and I don't pretend to have seen it all. I recently talked to my first transsexual donor. She is a woman who donated sperm years ago. She wants to meet her donor kids, but the mom on the other end isn't so sure. This donor faces some of the same issues I deal with every day, but with a twist.

Another recent first-case scenario is the story of a mom who always suspected that her fraternal twin children came from two different sperm donors. Back in the 1970s her clinic inseminated two days in a row (not uncommon), with two different donors (uncommon), and a recent DNA test confirmed her suspicion. Her kids are twins conceived with different biological fathers.

I talk a lot about redefining family, but that doesn't mean finding new definitions as much as being comfortable leaving definitions behind. I'm not sure there's a word for my relationship with Lance today. I care about him and want him to be happy. He is my son's biological father. We're not quite friends ... but sort of. We're not quite relatives ... but sort of. My bond with Fin was special and deeply felt but likewise without category. When people ask Ryan, "What is Lance to you? Is he like a dad, an uncle, a cousin, a friend?" Ryan answers, "It's like all of those and none of those. It's just a unique relationship." This has been typical of the experiences I've seen unfold through the DSR: It has turned out to be a vehicle to foster the development of all sorts of unique and very special relationships.

But there has been a troubling side as well. As our community grew over the years and more voices were heard, stories surfaced on the DSR of sperm banks and egg clinics not being honest, not keeping records, and ignoring important medical information coming from donor recipients, offspring, and donors. I began to wrap my head around the state of the donor industry, and I realized I could not be just a neutral observer. This growing awareness and understanding of the malpractice within the industry allowed me to become an advocate for donor families.

I regularly present our findings at legal conferences, LGBTQ events, medical and law schools, bioethics meetings, and reproductive medicine conferences like ASRM and ESHRE, but it still feels like an uphill battle. In the early days, they brushed us off, claiming that our data was merely "anecdotal." Then the DSR started partnering with prestigious researchers and institutions around the world such as the University of Cambridge to conduct and publish research on the parents (egg, sperm, and non-bio), egg and sperm donors, offspring, and even the donor-grandparents. We've now published more than two dozen papers in numerous peer-reviewed academic journals, and we'll continue to present our findings at conferences around the world.

It's vital that the rights, experiences, and concerns of donor-conceived individuals continue to be introduced as topics of discussion at these conferences and in conversations despite the industry's continued resistance. At many reproductive medicine conferences, Ryan is the first donor-conceived person these medical professionals have ever met, yet these "experts" are setting policies that greatly affect the lives of donor-conceived individuals and their loved ones. The donor industry and medical community's focus is on selling gametes and helping people to become pregnant, often without much thought to the children they're helping to create. We try very hard to get them to understand the importance of properly educating and counseling the parents and the donors at the front door of the sperm bank or egg clinic, as they're making crucial decisions.

Progress within the industry is creeping at a snail's pace because profit nearly always comes before ethics. The donor industry is still the Wild West of medicine, with no laws in place to provide proper oversight or regulation—a situation that has resulted in many deeply disturbing reports from families. I hear all too often about sperm banks' unethical and irresponsible behavior resulting in an unacceptably high number of donor children with genetic diseases and with discoveries that the donor or the sperm bank was not honest about medical issues and history.

In most cases, medical information is neither updated nor shared with the families. A few years ago, Ryan tried to get California Cryobank to share some important medical information with his unknown half-siblings, and they flat-out refused. Other sperm banks have promised to share urgent medical information but have not done so. Some facilities continue to sell vials of sperm from donors who have been reported with genetic health issues. Many medical conditions are genetic in origin; some with environmental triggers. So, it can be extremely important in maintaining health and managing one's healthcare to know the diseases to which you or your child may have a predisposition. Only then can you remain on the lookout for possible symptoms, take precautionary treatment, and stay current on appropriate screenings.

All sperm banks still sell every vial of sperm as "anonymous," be it for 18 years or forever, but this is something that simply shouldn't be promised or expected. Similarly, given that accurate records are not being kept on the children born for any one donor, limits on the number of donor recipients should never be promised. We've learned that there are numerous potential psychological, social, and medical challenges for the offspring in the large half-sibling groups. For some, awareness of even a relatively small half-sibling group of a dozen might seem overwhelming. For the majority of parents, donor-conceived people, and donors, reckoning with the knowledge that your group of half-siblings contains 50 or 100 individuals (or even more) can be extremely challenging.

In a 2019 Stat News article, California Cryobank's spokesperson Scott Brown said, "I think it's a very selfish act to try and locate an unknown donor." He's clearly deeply invested in keeping donor-conceived people from connecting with their biological parents. This makes sense from his perspective, as these connections often reveal dishonest and unethical sperm bank industry practices. A month later, in an NBC news story, Scott was quoted again: *"Family is what we are in the business of, not genetic connection." As if the genetic connection between a mother and her child wasn't* exactly *what they're selling.* The fact is, genetic connections are important for donor-conceived individuals, not just between them and the family raising them but also between them and their donor family. DNA isn't the *only* way to define a family, but it is certainly *one* way. The families that buy gametes are acknowledging the importance of at least half of a genetic connection to the child they're about to create; otherwise, many of them would adopt instead.

But this is the sperm bank industry's "story," and they're sticking to it—despite decades of hearing from all stakeholders, including donors and donor-conceived people, about the importance of these connections, and despite dozens of research studies and papers published on the psychological importance for a person to know about their ancestry, medical background, and close genetic relatives. Donor-conceived people signed no agreements, and no one can deny that it's an innate human desire to know where we come from.

Over the years, the sperm banks have ignored, dismissed, and negated the work of the DSR. At one point, California Cryobank even tried to purchase the DSR for $150,000, promising to keep me on as a director, but indicating that they would install a board of directors that would monitor my work and my voice. That just wasn't going to happen. There is a lot of policy work still to be done, and we need the freedom to report the state of affairs accurately and honestly.

Because there has never been a need to be concerned about the health risks of sperm donors, we've been able to focus on the psychological and emotional experiences they may have. But we have learned through our research studies that there are additional issues with egg donors that deserve a lot more research. We've heard from many egg donors via the DSR and through our research studies, and it is now clear that there are both known and unknown medical risks, but egg donors have never been viewed as patients—only as sources of eggs. We know of egg donors who have experienced medical problems such as severe ovarian hyper-stimulation syndrome (OHSS), infertility, and cancer, yet the long-term risks of egg donation have not been adequately studied. It is important that this type of research happens as soon as possible. Egg donors should be making educated decisions informed by research into how donating might affect their current and future health.

There is at least one bright development that has occurred in the egg donation industry: More than two dozen egg clinics are now writing the DSR into their egg donation contracts so that parents and donors are connecting on the DSR right from pregnancy or birth. The parents and donors can then share emails, photos, and medical information, all while remaining private to each other if they so wish. But they can also meet up at Starbucks if they wish. This empowers both parties to determine the nature of their relationship without a middleman working hard to keep them from each other. This development is clearly in the best interests of the child being born, but not a single sperm bank has yet been willing to adopt this policy.

Epilogue

The Donor Sibling Registry has always been about educating, connecting, and supporting all those in the donor family. It's important for donors, parents, and offspring to know that they are not alone in their experience. Our donor family stories connect us to one another. It's important for everyone to know that there is a large community of people beside them, many who have walked the path that they're on, and who have survived and thrived. My goal has always been to serve this community of families well, to share my knowledge and experience as the mom of a donor child and as a professional in the field in a way that helps others to find their way. Building any family—but especially a donor family—is a difficult, messy, joyful, and rewarding endeavor.

Perhaps because so much had been broken within my own family, including the loss of three family members in a car accident when I was 19, it became crucial for me to try and repair the gaps within my son's unknown family so that it, and he, would be somehow less broken or incomplete. Also, it was extremely important to me that even when Ryan didn't know where 50% of him came from, he would always feel 100% complete and his curiosities would not only be heard but also be acknowledged and honored.

A question I frequently get is, "Would you have been honest with Ryan about his origins if you had stayed married?" It's a good question. Because Dan and I were honest with everyone about the donor conception, I can only assume that we would have continued on with this same honesty as we raised Ryan together. It's hard to imagine that I would have, at some point, decided to put the genie back in the bottle and proceeded by keeping the information secret.

It's hard to say just how different Ryan would be if he had never gotten the answers to the questions he was asking about his own paternal ancestry and relatives. I have heard from enough adult donor-conceived people to know that living without those answers can be extremely painful and challenging. I know that my life would have been less interesting, meaningful, and rich if not for Lance, Fin, and Don's presence, along with the half-siblings we've gotten to know along the way. These relationships have strengthened my resolve to keep working to make these types of connections possible for all stakeholders within the donor family.

Epilogue

As the landscape shifts and people find novel ways to define these new relationships, and as our families expand, the DSR will be here to help empower all of the stakeholders. Parents and donors should be properly educated and counseled at the front door of their doctor's office, egg clinic, or sperm bank, as the decisions they make early on will affect the children they're creating for decades to come. And donor-conceived individuals need a place where they can advocate for themselves and get the answers they truly deserve. Together we can take our common knowledge and experience and create a future that promotes more open, honest, and transparent donor families and a more ethical and responsible donor conception industry.

Acknowledgements

Thank you to Ellen Glazer, who via many long phone calls collected my story and then wrote the original article on which this memoir is based, and to Jennifer Schneider for her encouragement to make the story my own.

Thanks to Jane Constantineau and Helen Chang at Author Bridge Media for the additional phone chats and editing to help turn Ellen's article from third-person to first-person, and for helping to take my life experiences and turn them into the beginnings of this book. Additional editing thanks to Robert Hamilton and to Lavon Peters for both editing and publishing assistance.

About the Author

Wendy Kramer has co-authored many published papers on donor conception, has reviewed abstracts for the American Society of Reproductive Medicine, and has also been a peer reviewer for the journals *Human Reproduction, Reproductive BioMedicine Online,* and the *Journal of Comparative Effectiveness Research.* She was Associate Producer on the Style Network's 2011 Emmy-nominated show *Sperm Donor* and on MTV News & Docs 2013 docu-series *Generation Cryo.* Wendy and her son Ryan have appeared on *60 Minutes, Oprah, Good Morning America,* and many other news shows and publications. Wendy is co-author of the book *Finding Our Families: A First-of-Its-Kind Book for Donor-Conceived People and Their Families* and author of the children's book *Your Family: A Donor Kid's Story.* Wendy holds a B.A. from Long Island University.

You can contact Wendy via email at wendy@donorsiblingregistry.com, or visit the Donor Sibling Registry website: www.donorsiblingregistry.com.

www.ingramcontent.com/pod-product-compliance
Lightning Source LLC
Chambersburg PA
CBHW021957290426
44108CB00012B/1114